THE POEMS OF CATULLUS

THE POEMS OF CATULLUS

TRANSLATED
AND
WITH
AN
INTRODUCTION
BY

HORACE GREGORY

GROVE PRESS, INC.   NEW YORK

First Grove Press Edition 1956

Eighth Printing

Manufactured in the United States of America

INTRODUCTION

I

THE BOOK that follows the pages of this introduction was
written nearly thirty years ago. Its original author, the
source of its inspiration, was born near Verona in 84 B.C. and
died thirty years later in Rome. There are certain distances
here of time and place, and first of all, I must speak of its
more recent author, myself, who was younger than Catullus
at his death. To do so is to explain why I have not revised
the poems in this collection: truly enough they were written
by someone I know with plausible authority, but he who
wrote them was scarcely the same writer I am today. I would
rather not meddle with his lines even if I feel today that I
could improve them. The book is his version in English of
Catullus—and who am I to cramp his style, to stay his hand,
to stand over him as a father might, scold, praise and emend
him? His rights were well earned, and some of them have
the instinctive authority of a young poet: more than that, I
have no desire to lose his friendship. I have a profound
distrust of poets who in their later years are perpetually
quarreling with their younger selves. If they emend early
weaknesses (as Yeats did in the last edition of his *Collected
Poems*) it is best to do so quietly, and like Yeats to leave
discoveries of their emendations to their critics.

But why did this young man of American birth find an
affinity with a Veronese poet who died more than two thousand years ago? That was a question asked by the young
man's New York acquaintances. The young man's own poetry

had the external look of being very "modern": its people, its visual imagery, its associations, its incidents were of New York, New York of the late nineteen-twenties, its squalor and violence, the pathos and confusion of lives spent in offices and hotels, the restless brilliance of their futility, lives damned by the inaccessibility of ethics, God and love. What had such concerns to do with "classical affairs," particularly those of a well-to-do young Veronese who emulated what he had read of Sappho and Callimachus and had come down from Cisalpine Gaul to Rome? The young American in New York had made something of the same venture in leaving behind him a provincial city in the Middle West; the shock and excitement of landing in New York, the easternmost, almost European capital of the United States, were nearly as great as those of traveling down from Verona into Rome. This analogy is clear enough, and should be understood by all who never weary of reminding us that New York is NOT America, for even today Verona no more resembles Rome than Indianapolis or Milwaukee has the contours of New York. Yet my impulse to write a new version of Catullus had far deeper roots than this analogy.

The deeper roots had their sources in the peculiar, closely guarded family circle out of which the young man came. It was of Anglo-Irish Dublin-London origins set down remotely in a German-American city. Within the family all conversation retained a Dublin accent, including faint undertones of an eighteenth-century Latinity. So strong was this heritage from a Trinity College Dublin grandfather that as a child I had difficulty making myself understood whenever I went out on errands to a corner bakery. As the red-faced German girl behind the counter stooped to hand me a paper bag filled with breakfast rolls, she said smiling, "You're a foreigner, ain't you? You come from someplace far east of here." Only embarrassment mixed with family pride restrained me from telling her that I had been born a few blocks away, and that fifteen years before that crucial date, my grandfather, friend of the city's first mayor and the city's first civil engineer, had died of old age, of boredom and bad real estate investments after laying out the city. To his family he left that curious, unearned heritage of family pride that only the Anglo-Irish can bestow, a kind of gentility that without the means of being smartly dressed, somehow achieved the look of precarious, almost fantastic elegance. It was an elegance, along with its Latinity, that leaned backward to the days of George IV, Maria Edgeworth and the last fading memories of Robert Emmet. "When my country takes its place among the nations of the earth" was recited oftener in my household than "The Gettysburg Address," and instructions for the rearing of children were taken from the titles and subtitles of Miss Edgeworth's *Parents' Assistance,* which included such precepts as "waste not, want not," or "two strings to your bow" —a reminder that was extremely difficult for an Anglo-Irish household to obey, for as my grandfather once wrote, his sons were "naturally extravagant," a gift that proved his own paternity. Not to know Latin in that household was to confess a loss of family pride, for it also admitted an inability to laugh at the Regency jokes in a comic Latin grammar that was a treasured book in my grandfather's library. Yet it was considered a disgrace to take instruction from sources outside the family library; to do so was a sign of being "a mental cripple."

In a German-American community, the sons of that grandfather created an island sufficient for themselves; the peculiarities of family speech and family legend were boldly cherished. During the American Civil War family neutrality had been maintained though some members fought for the cause of the Confederacy while others fought for the North; the war was less important than the existence of a family tree whose roots revealed a kinship to King Duncan and the Royal MacAlpin, the MacGregor sign of a lion who wore a crown. If in a middle western city some members of the clan failed to get the recognition they deserved—that was the world's misfortune, not the clan's. Such errors could be set down to Germanic ignorance or the thoughtlessness of egocentric Americans. At family dinners Regency formalities prevailed: Pope, Byron and Landor were quoted as frequently as Shakespeare. At my birth, an aunt remembered Horace, most likely by the way of rereading Pope's *Imitations of Horace,* and since she assumed the offices of a godmother, gave me my name: "Horace Victor Gregory has a lovely Latin sound," said she.

It was the Regency custom in that household for male members of the family to spend two hours at dressing in the morning; freshly bathed, tailored, starched and pressed, they began formalities at six-thirty at the breakfast table. What need there was to dazzle the eyes of so-called ignorant German businessmen I do not know, but I suspect that the less wealthy descendants of the Royal MacAlpin felt compelled to outshine, in dress at least, their more prosperous neighbors. The custom had one advantage: it succeeded in completely overlooking Victorian manners and clung to its original affinities. My father loathed Tennyson and reread Smollett, and though he hated Socialism, Bernard Shaw was the only modern writer he admired: "The man can write good plays," he said, "there is no nonsense in them." If Shaw was self-taught, so was he: at fourteen he had mastered the Latin grammars and laughed at the comic one in his father's library. It was an admission of failure on my part to go to prep school to learn my Caesar and Cicero (both of which threw me into

agonies) under the eyes of an ironic young Scot from Edin-
burgh. In those days, mathematics and Latin were my twin
terrors.

Though I no less than the next boy deeply hated grinding,
seemingly unrewarding labors, the achievement of the nearly
impossible has always held a perverse attraction for me;
therefore at college I steered my way toward calculus—
which created fears not unlike those of mountain climbing—
and Latin. The translator of Lucretius, the violent, kindly
Puritan divine who had disguised himself as a gray-haired
Shelley, a Devil's Disciple if there ever was one—William
Ellery Leonard—was my advisor. He taught me Anglo-
Saxon, as the course was named in the college catalogue, but
as he taught it Anglo-Saxon was merely one of the tongues
he spoke in giving lectures: Greek, Latin, German, Icelandic,
Hebrew dropped like so much red-hot lava from his lips;
even graduate students seldom passed his examinations. To
save my self-respect and to achieve the near impossible again,
I reinforced my position by reading Horace and Catullus
under the most brilliant of Leonard's colleagues, who hap-
pened to be on a year's absence from The American Acad-
emy at Rome. He was Moses Slaughter, who, sixty years
before he put an arm around me and steered me into his
classroom, had been born on a farm in Iowa. During the
intervening years he had become one of those American
middle westerners who are more European than any European I ever met: his dress, his look, his manner—he never
failed to wear a freshly cut flower in the lapel buttonhole of
a gray flannel jacket—bore a resemblance to photographs of
Edward VII. He seldom sat down to lecture—he walked, he
paced, he strolled about the room, then turning to where I sat
would recite softly:

> *"Acmen Septimios suos amores*
> *tenens in gremios 'mea' inquit 'Acme,*
> *ni te perdite amo atque amare porro*
> *omnes sum assidue paratus annos . . .*

Ah, that is love! What are you reading, Horace? Let me have
a decent English version of that poem tomorrow: drop it in
the postbox."

His class was small. As with Leonard's classes, no more
than four or five students were adventurous enough to face
the grim examinations and long term papers that followed
them, but at the year's end the only mark of academic dis-
tinction I received at college came from Slaughter because I
had converted one of Horace's odes into English metrics
which closely, if stiffly, approximated the original. Catullus
and Horace bolstered me sufficiently to get a passing grade
in Leonard's polylingual Anglo-Saxon; I had successfully
climbed, not without scars, that volcanic mountain. Mean-
while Slaughter's formalities in dress and manner, which
made him seem a snob to other students, reminded me of
formalities at home. When he invited me out to dinner, I felt
at ease with him, all the more so because I had the family
gift of being "extravagant," and paying for my own dinner
often meant overdrawing my allowance beyond midnight
hopes of settling my debts. When, two years later, I heard
of Slaughter's death in Rome, I thought of Ezra Pound's lines
from "Moeurs Contemporaines":

> They will come no more,
> The old men with beautiful manners.

Years later in the Protestant Cemetery at Rome I gazed at the
tablet over Slaughter's grave; his was a friendly ghost: I had
the conviction that his spirit was at rest:

> *in perpetuum . . . ave atque vale*

During my efforts to supply Slaughter with decent English

versions of Latin verse, I looked at those done by poets I admired. The search led me back in time, through Tennyson and Pope to Marvell, Herrick and Campion, until I came to a "discovery" of Ben Jonson. It was all too obvious that I had much to learn, but Jonson's adaptations from the ancients provided a model so very high above my reach that it could never seem ordinary or grow stale. His example was an inspiration to go my own way as best I could; the same general directions were likewise pointed by Ezra Pound's *Homage to Sextus Propertius.* It was my belief that Catullus lacked a twentieth-century interpreter; in his own right, he was tremendously alive, but much unread. Since absolute translation of poetry from one language to another has always been notoriously impossible, the near impossible again offered me its temptations; I also was convinced that however far short of perfection some of my adaptations fell, the results would not be mediocre—in short my Catullus would not be mistaken as the author of verses published in popular magazines.

But now it is time to speak of Catullus himself, rather than of what I was some thirty years ago.

II

Behind the poems of Catullus there is a story that has been retold many times. The latest version of it may be found in Thornton Wilder's novel *The Ides of March,* but most of its details have been known to British schoolboys since the sixteenth century. Catullus, the second son of a wealthy army contractor stationed in Cisalpine Gaul, was born and educated in and near Verona. There he came under the influence of the teachings of Valerius Cato, a brilliant Hellenist who carried the torch of Greek studies into the provinces of

Rome; it is probable that the poet was tutored by one of Cato's pupils. It was in Cato's circle that Catullus moved, and there within a group of promising young intellectuals, poets, politicians, lawyers, he was the acknowledged genius, the desired lover, the all-night drinker, and good friend. Among his friends were Furius Bibaculus, Gaius Licinius Calvus, Veranius, Fabullus, Cinna the poet, Quintilius Varus the critic, Cornelius the soldier, Manlius Torquatus the aristocrat, and Marcus Caelius Rufus, the good-looking, fair-haired rake and politician. The group were of a fashionable set who hated the rising Julius Caesar and underrated his social charm as well as his potential statesmanship; a few of them were young friends of Cicero. All lived with violent intensity, exchanging either girls or boys as lovers. No one doubted the superior talents of the group, and "dissipation" was a mild word to describe their nights and days. Since most of them were very rich young men, the sordid aspect of all they said was glazed by the opaque surfaces of being in high fashion; they "glittered when they walked." In the looking glass of Catullus' poems their high fashion has endured, and they reflect the untarnished brightness of a culture that was less Greek than Roman and less strictly Roman in its high lights than Veronese.

Into this circle flashed Clodia, wife of the heavy-minded governor of Cisalpine Gaul. She was related by marriage and descent to two of the most ancient and highly respected senatorial families in Rome; she was willfully naughty, and it was rumored after her husband's death that in a fit of boredom she had poisoned him and had resumed the pleasure of sleeping with her brother. She was nearly five years older than Catullus. Aside from the poems Catullus wrote and Cicero's polemic against her in a courtroom, no portrait of this Circe in Roman undress exists, but she may well have looked something like the Venus Veronese imagined, who, flushed and cheerful on a wall of the Metropolitan Museum in New York, is just about to be embraced by Mars.

It is believed that in 62 B.C. Catullus followed Clodia, the "Lesbia" of his poems, down to Rome, and it is assumed that there she led him through a labyrinth of pleasures and disillusionments. That from her he contracted a touch of madness may be believed, but the spell was broken temporarily by the shock of hearing that his brother had died on a diplomatic mission to Asia Minor. Catullus, with a few friends, entered the service of Memmius Gemellus, proconsul to Bithynia. He stayed in Bithynia a year, and then, impelled by boredom and a longing for Italy, sailed in his own yacht around the shores of Greece and through the Adriatic back to Verona. Still restless, he returned to Rome, where the old madness tinged by distrust and hatred began again. Shortly after his return came death, and here—there are no reports of a deathbed scene or how death came—the Catullus story ends.

But the entire story, or rather the fragments of the story that we know are seen in the amber-colored light of an Italian evening. The characters who live within the story remain untouched by middle age; none has lived long enough to bore his sons and daughters with memoirs of how wicked he once was; none is afflicted with palsy or arthritis; none suffers the slow mind and speech and the quick irrational rage of dipsomania; none lies awake counting a slow pulse beat and with it all the fears of hypochondria. None lectures on what he might have been. The charm of the brief story is its immediacy, and associated as it is with the poems of Catullus, the youthful characters even today live in the present tense. I suspect that Catullus and his friends, including Clodia, had made a cult of youth, and that within that circle, sex and madness, art, beauty, grief, guilt, slander, even murder were accepted as the order of the day or night. For us, at least, the scene without Catullus at its center would soon grow stale or empty; and if not dull, its colors would fade into the chromos of the feature story that is published every week in Sunday editions of tabloid newspapers. The Catullus circle has a passing analogy to groups that formed and dissolved so quickly during the nineteen-twenties in the United States. The Cult of Youth rode high and was indulged; "speakeasies" thrived; the foolish, brutal side of living was turned uppermost; millions were made, inherited, and spent; unmentionable things were said and forgotten. Italian gangsters, "public enemies," either "One" or "Two," were jailed for nonpayment of income taxes (not for their true crimes) or shot down by rivals. These characters were young men; even young intellectuals from Princeton, Yale or Harvard, who never owned a gun and would fear to touch one, aped gangster methods in forming literary groups and tried to emulate the conduct of James Cagney in a gangster film. So far, the story behind the poems of Catullus has an analogy to the sensational surfaces of life in twentieth-century America. Today the public surface has another face: the teen-age gangster has arrived and men and women past the age of fifty (vaguely nostalgic for the nineteen-twenties) dress up in teen-age sportswear and shield their eyes with large sun-goggles.

III

The story behind Catullus' poems cannot be given as the mirror of all they have to say; it cites a few sources of their inspiration. The story gives us certain points of reference, but does not account for the poetic genius that makes them memorable. The relation of the story to the poems is the same that joins the facts of W. B. Yeats' life to his early poems: Maud Gonne disguised as Helen of Troy has the same being as Clodia disguised as Lesbia, which is to say both ladies have undergone a metamorphosis; their immortality is a gift conferred upon them by a young poet. How far that metamorphosis may change the original is indicated by the legend of George Moore's remark to Yeats apropos of Maud Gonne's tall stature: "Willie, I would just as soon go to bed with a British grenadier as sleep with Maud Gonne" and Yeats did not like (which was never much) George Moore the better for his opinion. Lesbia was the image of what Catullus knew and felt—the image of love which always carries with it a trace of the self-image, a shadow of the shadow Narcissus saw below him in the pool. Poets in writing of their ladies seldom give us the colors of the lady's eyes and hair; or if they are called to name them, they transform them to colors suiting the intensity of their emotion toward the lady. During the Renaissance Italian writers of the sestina and the sonnet took, as a courtly habit, the image of a lady to signify ideas as well as passions, and poets of the English Renaissance took their examples from Italian masters. It is said that Anne Boleyn inspired one of Sir Thomas Wyatt's English adaptations of Petrarch; perhaps she did, but the sonnet gives us rather an example of Wyatt's wit, half concealed in the image of courtly love. So I could go on citing a long list of mutations from the woman herself to her image in the poem; Romantic poets, German, English and French, rediscovered her, and Leopardi, whose sexual experiences with women were notoriously nonexistent, wrote poems in which the images of girls and women have an air of timelessness.

Yet it would be a mistake to regard Catullus' Lesbia in the same light as the image of a woman in Symbolist poetry, particularly in the poetry of the later Yeats and of Alexander Blok. There is an important shade of difference here. Catullus' Lesbia is more strictly the image of love, of love that fixes its image in the lover's eye and then possesses him with madness, a madness which flows through his veins and which may exalt him to godhead or consume him utterly. This kind of image takes for granted a powerful affinity between the poet and the object of his love, and it is here that the shadow of Narcissus plays its destructive part. Whatever charms Catullus' Lesbia possessed, those spells were equaled by the poems he wrote of her in company with her sparrow; poet and mistress share the magic of those moments, even to the light touch of grief when the sparrow dies. It is Catullus' way of saying how completely he is charmed. The same evocation of a spell enters his adaptation of one of Sappho's lyrics, but with a deeper hint of being trapped by the very magic exchanged between the lovers. The same note of enchantment enters his play of wit in the poem describing an exchange of kisses. Lesbia yields to his tastes and he to hers; the evil side of the relationship is still concealed; only its madness, its self-consuming dangers, come to light. (As for Clodia, the lady behind the scene, she resembled Catullus in being at the center of each room she entered; in this at least they held equality. Both in equal measure enjoyed the trick of making her husband a victim of adultery; they were of one mind in the exercise of that kind of wit; it increased the sense of danger in their pleasures. To this degree, Catullus' Lesbia is faithful, though faithful in nothing else, to her original.)

The disillusionment of the poet with his Lesbia is a natural sequel to the madness which possessed him; time came when the madness wore an opposing mask of hatred, yet the fascination of Lesbia remained. The spell of Circe could be broken, yet since Catullus was not Ulysses—lacking his mother wit, the friendship of Minerva—the poet returned to his Lesbia and Rome. It has been argued that Catullus innocently chose the name "Lesbia" for his heroine; as I reread him, I think not. His poem to Juventius shows clearly enough his understanding of homosexual relationships, nor did he, I think, read Sappho with the unpractised eye of a boy brought up on a New England farm. Italian boys of his temperament and generation may have been innocent enough in forming judgments of their friends, but in matters of sexual behavior they were notoriously adroit. And we already know that Catullus' wealth and education were of a kind that banished ignorance in the pursuit of pleasure. He was, moreover, two thousand years closer to Sappho's world than we are today. His choice of the name "Lesbia" has several undertones of meaning: some may have been, so far as he was concerned, subconscious, others with a very light turn of ironic wit, some with the obvious meaning of acknowledging a literary debt to Sappho, some as a compliment to Clodia— and anyhow, remembering always that Catullus is a lyric poet of the first order, the name "Lesbia" has a decidedly attractive liquid sound. As to the probable subconscious or instinctive meanings, Lesbia becomes as bisexual as he; she is unfaithful to her heavy-minded husband, which provides for a play of wit; and there is a possible compliment implied in that Lesbia's beauty, taste, and intelligence would meet the approval of Sappho herself. These reasons are enough to make his choice of "Lesbia" appropriate to what he had to say, and the name probably came to him as an inspiration from Apollo.

The charm of the love lyrics extends throughout the collection rescued from manuscripts dating back to the ninth century; scholars have quarreled over the order in which certain poems have been presented, but few dispute the spell they cast upon the reader. Some are exercises, notably the poem on Berenice's hair, and the possibility is great that the poems celebrating marriage were written in homage to what Catullus learned from Sappho, and these epithalamiums are among the best of Catullus' poems. There has always been some difficulty in explaining why Catullus in the many ages that followed his has seemed so "modern" to each: why, for instance, John Skelton in Henry VIII's day felt inspired to write his supremely gay "Philip Sparrow" with the thought of Lesbia's sparrow urging his hand. This is one out of many instances, but other extremes of inspiration exist among the poems of Crashaw and Coleridge; to name all the poets (in English alone) who have adapted a poem or two of Catullus would begin to rival the list of names covering a page of the New York telephone directory. Each century since Skelton's day has more than passively accepted Catullus' small collection of poems as being relevant to its own time. Is the reason to be found in his art alone? Not quite. Is it in his situation within a circle that made a cult of youth? Again, not quite. Is it because some of his poems reveal for each age a singular penetration into the psychology of sex? Not quite: although these reasons have their bearing on the nature of Catullus' poetry.

The secret is, I think, in the timeless, yet *immediate* effect the poems have upon the reader: in the majority of the poems, the veil of writing, even the printed page, seem to drop away between the reader and the poet. In all forms of literature that kind of contact is extremely rare, and that is why, to the reader of English poetry, Catullus' poems, though written in an age called "classical," create the illusion of being "romantic." In this Catullus shared the secret (hinted at from what little we know of her poems) possessed by

Sappho: art, plus the mysterious x, the indefinable quality of candor which illuminates all images of life within the poem. That is why nineteenth-century critics found in the last stanza of Catullus' poem XI an analogy to Robert Burns's "Lines To A Daisy"; but Catullus' sapphics are more compact, are better turned, and have deeper emotional resonance within themselves than Burns's stanzas. Burns, of course, was not influenced by Catullus; he came by direct observation to the image of a flower being overturned by a plow; whatever "classical" influences he had came from a close reading and rereading of Alexander Pope, nor could he have chosen a better master to guide his genius; his other great debt was to his near contemporary, James Fergusson, whose life was briefer than Catullus' and his own.

Catullus' great gift was that of revealing the essentials of his psyche, the gift of writing directly of what he felt and knew. He was not given to speculation: his metaphysics began and ended with poems V, *Vivamus, mea Lesbia,* and VII, *Quaeris, quot mihi basiationes,* and with the exceptions of poems LXVI (his version of a poem by Callimachus) LXVIII (b) and LXIII, the spell that he created was one of an eternal present tense. His gift was aided by a kind of insight that so often shocks the northern European and the American when both encounter the Italian; in earthly matters—sex, the enjoyment of food and money—the Italians, ancient or modern, tend to be what we call "practical"; they are masters of a way of life that takes each moment as it comes, and are wide-eyed and unashamed of being so. They are instinctive opportunists, happy when Fortuna smiles down at them, and deeply disquieted when she does not. Anyone who misreads such reactions as childishness had better change his mind, for it is a way of living that carries within it great capacities of endurance. So far as Catullus' own life was concerned, boredom seems to have driven him to the extremes of reck-lessness, even to probable self-destruction; but in his poems, the moment—whether he was in love or out of love, whether in grief, or the delight of friendship, whether in hate or the madness of jealousy—the passing moment was his to live. Therefore his poems are less "romantic" than at times they seem to be; they do not look backward, but seem to absorb and then illuminate the trials or pleasures of an immediate occasion. We do not know, of course, how long he took to write a poem; we are fairly certain that he polished it before he selected it as one of the hundred and fifteen other poems in his book. Whatever he at the moment loved, he celebrated; and what hated the moment after, wrote of with equal vehe-mence; nor did he intend, I think, to write an autobiography: his record was one of his more intense emotions, the play of his wit and ability to charm. Though it is known Julius Caesar, as he could well afford to do, outcharmed Catullus and won the poet as a friend, the contra-Caesar poem remains in Catullus' collection. Was it inserted by one of the poet's friends? Perhaps. Or was it allowed to stand because it cap-tured so completely Catullus' feeling at the time he wrote it? I suspect that the answer is yes to the latter question.

IV

As the poems appear in the present English version, a long accepted conventional order is allowed to stand. The collated texts of seven manuscripts (*codex,* not the papyrus roll, *liber* of Catullus' day) have been in the hands of scholars since the fourteenth century, and the results of these readings are the sources of twentieth-century authorities, which means that since 1400 no major revisions have been made. Papyrus roll editions (and it is believed that what we now consider "the collected works" were in three separate papyrus rolls) were circulated in Rome during the first and second centuries A.D.: the proof is that they were read by the younger Pliny and admired by the poet Martial. The parchment book (*codex*) manuscripts were copies of the earlier papyrus rolls which have been lost. Whether these transcriptions from papyrus to parchment followed the sequence of three groups of poems as they were issued is, of course, unknown. A lack of evidence faces the well-wishing student who attempts to renumber the poems in chronological order. Is the order one of biographical events, using the Clodia story as a guide? Possibly. Or is the order one in which Catullus published the poems in their final versions? Did he, like Robert Herrick, many centuries after him, rewrite his poems, arranging them in the order of their final drafts as they were given to copyists? We know nothing of his working habits beyond his admiration for the Alexandrian school of Cato. Did later transcribers confuse his order? Perhaps, for human error is far more common than the exercise of poetic art.

All we can say is that the present order (with the exception of poem XI) roughly follows an order of psychological appeal. The deathless hymn to Diana seems like a poem written before Catullus came to Rome. The present order (whether Catullus had a hand in it or not) might have been worse. Taking it at its best, the "showpieces," the poems exerting the greatest charm, introduce the collection, including the disarming foreword to the book. The longer poems **near the** center of the book act as ballast, as though the entire collection resembled the structure of a yacht, cutting through the waters of the Adriatic. Of the longer poems the marriage hymns are notably the best, and they were, it now seems certain, inspired by Sappho. The book closes with the elegy to his brother, followed by a scattering of epigrams, last words, as though the poet were consumed, burnt-out by the fires of his inspiration. There is no doubt that Poem XI should have been placed (as far as chronological order may be respected) last.

V

Last words are also in order for the English version of this book as it was written thirty years ago. My first guide in writing it was Ben Jonson, poet and matchless Latinist; and as I said earlier, I had much to learn, nor could I hope to rival him. I still believe I chose the best of masters. But I had also been reading other guides who were closer to me in time: one book was Ezra Pound's *Homage to Sextus Propertius,* and others were stray writings of D. H. Lawrence, not the short stories, but the marvelous travel sketches with Italian settings and with them a few of the later, unrhymed poems he wrote in Italy. How deeply these writers "influenced" me I do not know, nor did I attempt to rival them, but they served the great purpose of leading me away from nineteenth-century "classroom" standards in writing my adaptations from Catullus. They were neither leatherbound Latinists nor scholars in the conventional meanings of those terms, but are poets of the first order, different in kind from each other, and, for that matter, at some distance from Ben Jonson. Time is revealing both Pound and Lawrence as among the true "makers" of twentieth-century literature.

My purpose was to adapt, even if the venture seemed dangerously impossible, the immediate quality of Catullus' poems into English poetry, to make the reader feel that the hundred and sixteen poems that have been handed down to us under Catullus' name held a mirror up to life that could be read today. The work was done neither as a thesis nor for immediate rewards, but rather as an inspired necessity. Good fortune led me to a publisher who was also an editor and a friend of poets, Pascal Covici. He understood my reasons for writing an English version of all Catullus' poems: he accepted the risk of publishing a book of poems which had been inspired by a Veronese poet who died in 54 B.C.

After the book had been through two editions, it went out of print and became a rarity in book stores. Strangely high prices were offered for it; university librarians and students of Latin in colleges wrote letters to me asking where or how the book could be brought to light again. But I could not help them, for like most writers, I neglect to keep stocks of my books at hand; after I write them, they are the concern (I hope) of publishers and book sellers. For the past ten years book sellers themselves have been asking me where my Catullus could be found; when I would mention some catalogue where I had seen a listing of it, word would come back to me that the book had already been sold. Those who owned the book seldom released a copy to secondhand-book sellers. I began to feel that the book had a life of its own.

The present edition, unrevised, is one that comes to a new generation of readers. Catullus surely is as much alive today as he was in 1931 when the first edition of this book appeared. Rereading an English version of his poems today is, I think, as refreshing as ever, but it is never equal to the charm of Catullus' Latin: it is in the nature of poetry itself to belong to the language in which it is written. No translator or one who attempts the adaptation of a poem from one language to another should make the claim that his poem equals the original. All that the translator does is to acknowledge the source of his inspiration. He may be as literal as he pleases and still be desperately wrong. That is why some of the worthiest of scholars so often fail in giving us legible versions of poetry in translation: the mysterious *x*, the in-spired quality, is lacking; the necessary illumination of the original is gone. And this is particularly true of attempted translations into English from the Ancients. How to recapture the signs of life heard, seen and felt within a poem written over two thousand years ago is among the mysteries of inspiration. As I said before, the poems of Catullus have seemed "modern" in each of the six centuries that followed the thirteen hundred years after his death. But what of their appeal through the ages between the first century and 1400? They had been transcribed and read, actually preserved, by those who paid homage to the poet's genius, and this was through a period when many books of greater weight were mislaid or lost or deliberately destroyed. By singular good fortune, Catullus' poems fell into friendly hands. Their survival is in itself a monument.

THE POEMS OF
CATULLUS

I

QVI dono lepidum nouum libellum
arido modo pumice expolitum?
Corneli, tibi: namque tu solebas
meas esse aliquid putare nugas;
iam tum cum ausus es unus Italorum
omne aeuum tribus explicare cartis
doctis, Iuppiter, et laboriosis:
quare habe tibi quidquid hoc libelli
qualecumque; quod, o patrona uirgo,
plus uno maneat perenne saeclo.

1

WHO shall receive my new-born book,
my poems, elegant and shy,
neatly dressed and polished?

You, Cornelius,
shall be my single patron,
for, long ago, you praised
my slender lines and stanzas;

You, the only man in Italy
whose genius had the vigour
to write the history of the world
in three sturdy volumes;

These were books, by Jupiter,
that showed a learned mind and
the strength for heavy labour.

Then, take this little book
for what it is, my friend.

Patroness and Muse,
keep these poems green for
a day or so beyond a hundred years,

O Virgin!

SPARROW, O, sweet sparrow,
love of my lady love,
she who's always nursing
you between her breasts and
feeding you her finger-tips;
she, that radiant lady,
delicious in her play with you,
for a while forgetting
all the deeper wounds of love . . .
I envy her. This pastime
would raise my heart from darkness.

HERE is my relief at last,
not unlike the pleasure that came to the swift-footed
girl they call Atalanta, seizing the golden apple
that released her tiresome girdle.

LVGETE, o Veneres Cupidinesque,
et quantum est hominum uenustiorum.
passer mortuus est meae puellae,
passer, deliciae meae puellae.
quem plus illa oculis suis amabat:
nam mellitus erat suamque norat
ipsam tam bene quam puella matrem.
nec sese a gremio illius mouebat,
sed circumsiliens modo huc modo illuc
ad solam dominam usque pipilabat.
qui nunc it per iter tenebricosum
illuc, unde negant redire quenquam.
at uobis male sit, malae tenebrae
Orci, quae omnia bella deuoratis:
tam bellum mihi passerem abstulistis.
uae factum male! uae miselle passer,
tua nunc opera meae puellae
flendo turgiduli rubent ocelli.

3

DRESS now in sorrow, O all
you shades of Venus,
and your little cupids weep.

My girl has lost her darling sparrow;
he is dead, her precious toy
that she loved more than her two eyes,
O, honeyed sparrow following her
as a girl follows her mother,
never to leave her breast, but tripping
now here, now there, and always singing
his sweet falsetto
song to her alone.

Now he is gone; poor creature,
lost in darkness,
to a sad place
from which no one returns.

O ravenous hell!
My evil hatred rises against your power,
you that devour
all things beautiful;
and now this pitiful, broken sparrow,
who is the cause of my girl's grief,
making her eyes weary and red with sorrow.

THIS little yacht, look at her, O my friends,
was swift as wind, more speed in her
than any ship that sailed our seas; mast prow and stern
would pass all others, driven by
broad-bellied sail or winged with oars.

And these will verify her record:
the roaring Adriatic, islands in the Ægean,
familiar Rhodes, Thrace and its horrible shores,
treacherous Pontus gulf where once she stood
high in the forest overhead and spoke the language
of mount Cytorus, her speech all wind and leaves.

Believe her when she claims that she was one
with your green branches, this the place where she was born,
the very hills she saw above her when she sailed
violent seas circling Amastris,
oars speeding toward her master.

And if the wind came port or starboard,
or if Jove himself roared down both sheets at once,
and if (all innocent) she defied the gods
of time and chance, still she was fit
to weather distant oceans
and quiet lakes that welcomed her
at home. She sails no more, calm and old age

protect her; her remains are given
to Castor-Pollux, twins, the patron saints
whom all good sailors praise.

V

VIVAMVS, mea Lesbia, atque amemus,
rumoresque senum seueriorum
omnes unius aestimemus assis.
soles occidere et redire possunt:
nobis cum semel occidit breuis lux,
nox est perpetua una dormienda.
da mi basia mille, deinde centum,
dein mille altera, dein secunda centum,
deinde usque altera mille, deinde centum.
dein, cum milia multa fecerimus,
conturbabimus illa, ne sciamus,
aut ne quis malus inuidere possit,
cum tantum sciat esse basiorum.

5

COME, Lesbia, let us live and love,
nor give a damn what sour old men say.
The sun that sets may rise again
but when our light has sunk into the earth,
it is gone forever.

      Give me a thousand kisses,
then a hundred, another thousand,
another hundred
      and in one breath
still kiss another thousand,
another hundred.

      O then with lips and bodies joined
many deep thousands;
      confuse
their number,
      so that poor fools and cuckolds (envious
even now) shall never
learn our wealth and curse us
with their
evil eyes.

6

FLAVIUS, if your girl friend
were not a little bastard,
you'd be telling your Catullus
all about her charms forever.
Now I know the story:
she's some feverish little bitch
that's warm and sweet and dirty
and you can't get up the nerve
to tell me that you love her.
Not a word! Look at your bed
still trembling with your labours
(tell me that you sleep alone)
sheets soiled with love and flowers,
and why, why?
      Look at your poor loins
all bruised and empty.
No matter who she is or why,
I'll immortalize you
and your dear young lady
in a blushing blissful song
that echoes against heaven.

DO you know, my Lesbia, how many of your kisses
would satisfy my hunger? Count the sands of Africa
from Cyrene, famous for its spices,
from the place where Battus lies,
sepulchred and holy,
to the distant shrine where Jove's eloquence still smoulders;
count the constellations of the stars that rising through the
    silence
of night look down upon trembling furtive lovers:
then you will know how many times and more
your mad Catullus
could kiss you, kisses ripening beyond the calculation
of the curious eye, nor could a rapid envious tongue
gain speed to count their number.

8

POOR damned Catullus, here's no time for nonsense,
open your eyes, O idiot, innocent boy, look at what has
    happened:
once there were sunlit days when you followed after
where ever a girl would go, she loved with greater
love than any woman knew.
Then you took your pleasure
and the girl was not unwilling. Those were the bright days,
    gone;
now she's no longer yielding; you must be, poor idiot,
more like a man! not running after
her your mind all tears; stand firm, insensitive.
say with a smile, voice steady, "Good-bye, my girl,"
    Catullus
strong and manly no longer follows you, nor comes when
    you are calling
him at night and you shall need him.
You whore! Where's your man to cling to, who will praise
    your beauty,
where's the man that you love and who will call you his,
and when you fall to kissing, whose lips will you devour?
But always, your Catullus will be as firm as rock is.

9

VARANIUS, my dear, you're more to me than all my friends
within three hundred miles.
Are you once more surrounded
by those at home: your mother, now grown old,
and your harmonious brothers?
And this good news is true? and glorious news for me:
once more to see you sound and flourishing,
reciting vivid narratives of Spain
in your own fashion. Then shall I
draw you to me, kiss your mouth and eyes, O,
most fortunate, beloved of all men—
but who's more fortunate than I, filled with this riotous joy
at seeing you and greeting you again?

WHILE I was wandering, foot-loose, in the Forum,
Varus captured me and took me to his lady,
pretty little piece; at first sight, not bad looking,
nor did she lack refinement.
And there we talked a few words
of this and that. We spoke of
Bithynia, how that province looked and whether
my visit there had paid me.
I said (and this was truth) that neither governors nor
their retinues rolled in fat, nor richly fed, nor perfumed,
particularly since the chief, a filthy pervert,
refused to give a damn for those who served and helped
    him.
"Well anyhow" they said, "you must have had a servant
or two hoisting your litter, creatures like that are
bred in Bithynia." I answered: "I was better off than most
in that barren province with eight strapping fellows,
who carried me about."
        But I, of course, had no one,
not even a crippled slave to lift a broken bed on
    his shoulders.
        Then she, O shamelessly,
the barefaced little whore said: "My dear Catullus, please
let me have your men to take me to the temple of

Sarapis the Egyptian." I cried out "Stop, you go too
fast. Here's a mistake. These slaves are
not mine to offer ladies.

They happen to belong, in fact, to Gaius Cinna,
best friend I own; you see there is no difference
if slaves are his or mine. I use them on occasion,
but you, you little fool, eternal bore and nuisance,
will not allow a man a graceful turn of speech in
casual, delightful, and careless conversation."

XI

FVRI et Aureli, comites Catulli,
siue in extremos penetrabit Indos,
litus ut longe resonante Eoa
    tunditur unda,
siue in Hyrcanos Arabesque molles,
seu Sacas sagittiferosue Parthos,
siue quae septemgeminus colorat
    aequora Nilus,
siue trans altas gradietur Alpes,
Caesaris uisens monimenta magni,
Gallicum Rhenum horribilesque ulti-
    mosque Britannos,
omnia haec, quaecunque feret uoluntas
caelitum, temptare simul parati,
pauca nuntiate meae puellae
    non bona dicta.
cum suis uiuat ualeatque moechis,
quos simul complexa tenet trecentos,
nullum amans uere, sed identidem omnium
    ilia rumpens:
nec meum respectet, ut ante, amorem,
qui illius culpa cecidit uelut prati
ultimi flos, praetereunte postquam
    tactus aratro est.

11

FURIUS, Aurelius, bound to Catullus
though he marches piercing farthest India
where echoing waves of the Eastern Oceans
    break upon the shores:

Under Caspian seas, to mild Arabia,
east of Parthia, dark with savage bowmen,
or where the Nile, sevenfold and uprising,
    stains its leveled sands,—

Even though he marches over Alps to gaze on
great Caesar's monuments: the Gallic Rhine and
Britons who live beyond torn seas, remotest
    men of distant lands—

Friends who defy with me all things, whatever
gods may send us, go now, friends, deliver
these words to my lady, nor sweet—flattering,
    nor kind nor gentle:

Live well and sleep with adulterous lovers,
three hundred men between your thighs, embracing
all love turned false, again, again, and breaking
    their strength, now sterile.

She will not find my love (once hers) returning;
she it was who caused love, this lonely flower,
tossed aside, to fall by the plough dividing
    blossoming meadows.

ASINIUS MARRUCINUS you do not make a graceful
use of sleight of hand in stealing table linen;
if dinner guests are careless, do tricks like these show
    humour?
Fool! You're wrong, you're merely boorish.
And now you won't believe me and though Pollio your
    brother
would give up all his talents
to cure you of your vices. For he's a pretty fellow,
sweet, delicate, and faultless in all his blandishments.
I warn you now, three hundred
hendecasyllables shall follow you forever,
or, give me back my napkin;
its cost does not disturb me
but it's a present sent from my two friends (and priceless
this gift from Spain) these napkins, Fabullus
and Veranius gave to me; I treasure them, the symbol
of these dear friends and friendship.

13

COME, my Fabullus, there's a grand dinner waiting
for you at my house tomorrow, or the next day,
or the next, or a few days after—
that is, if gods are kind and you bring a banquet with
    you:
don't forget a round of wine and
a bright-eyed, sparkling girl and
your wit and every known variety of laughter.

Bring these, my dear, and you
shall have a glorious dinner;
your Catullus (see his purse)
has nothing left but cobwebs.
But if you look again, I'll give you something price-
    less—
friendship is here, my heart, richer
than love or passion.
Wait! Here's the perfume Venus
brought to my lovely lady with Cupids dancing round
    her;
friend Fabullus when you smell this rapture,
pray the gods to be
one great sensuous nose
forever!

IF I did not love you more, delightful Calvus,
more than my two eyes, my dear, I'd hate you
as much, O bitterly as we hate Vatinius.
Here's why: this gift you sent me, O what a gift,
why punish me? What's my offense? And have I ever hurt
    you,
giving you cause to torture me with these villainous poets?
I hope the gods will mutilate that client of yours who sent
    these
poets in a book to you, poor devils, damned forever.
Now I believe these poets, all new, no doubt, discovered
by Sulla and he gave them to you. I'm glad he paid you.
Your service is rewarded. Gods, what a foolish
heavy book it is. A gift to send Catullus
on a holiday and murder him with boredom.
No, no, you won't get off
so easily tomorrow. When tomorrow comes I'll clean out
the bookstores, group together
the works of Caesii, Aquini, the poems of Suffenus,
all these and other poets, filth and poison
to give you your full measure.
Good-bye, O poets, back into hell with you; crawl back
with crippled feet. You've brought disaster
to our times, O worst of modern poets.

14 (b)

IF there is anyone
who reads this foolishness,
do not fall back in horror, fear to put your
hands upon me,
O you who read these lines. . . .

15

I GIVE you, Aurelius,
all my love, my treasure;
and now I ask you, beg you
to do me a slight favour.
If ever you have valued anything
beyond all measure, held in your soul, Aurelius,
to guard it from disaster—
then guard this boy. O keep him
intact from all dishonour.

I do not fear the rabble
that walks the streets, nor those who
are absorbed in their own business—
it's you I fear, Aurelius,
for you are too attractive
to all young men both good and bad—
go, work your charms upon them,
leave this boy alone,
(for this I know is but the slightest favour
I ask of you). But if infatuation
drives you mad and you betray my lover,
I'll make my vengeance public.
You'll be in chains, a warning to all who pass the city
    gates,

and radishes and mullets all thrust between your
   buttocks,
a sign of your adultery, my good friend, Aurelius!

FURIUS, Aurelius, I'll work your own perversions
upon you and your persons, since you say my poems
prove that I'm effeminate, deep in homosexual
    vice.
A genuine poet must be chaste, industrious,
though his verse may give us
rich, voluptuous passion to please the
taste of those who read him and not only
delicate boys, but bearded men whose limbs are
stiff and out of practice. And you because my verses
contain many (thousands of) kisses, look at me
as though I were a girl. Come at me, and I'll be ready
to defile you and seduce you.

O COLONIA, O city,

       commemorate your festivals, with a wide bridge,
       a platform,

built for strength and dancing.

Your little bridge will crumble, trembling legs and all, vanish
       in mud and water—

make your bridge one fit for the mad fantastic dancing of the
       Salii who at Rome

re-awoke the thunder of their gods with dancing feet. O,
       Colonia my wish is

a bridge like this. And if it's built my laughter shall re-echo

all laughter. In Verona there's a fool whom

I'd like to see jump from your bridge into the deepest swamp
       that

your country has. This idiot, more foolish

than any fool, this old man (like a baby whining, shaking
       within its father's arms) has married

a girl who blooms like spring herself, more delicate and
       gentle than a young goat and playful.

Who should be cared for watchfully as ripened grapes, temp-
       tation

for any thief. But no, the fool is drowsy,

sleeps like a tree beside her, a tree struck down by axes,
       and fallen

into a ditch, hears not a thing, sees nothing nor knows if it's
                        alive or
dead. And that's the reason why your bridge will please me—
O to see him wake his head, his slow revolving mind in
                      darkest slime
held fast, there in bog, secure as
an iron shoe, left by a mule and sunken in black mire.

2 1

LISTEN, Aurelius, parsimonious, father
of famine that has struck the earth
in the past and future,
you are making love again to my boy, O
lick your lips and gaze at him, my love—
you sit beside him (no secret now), to tempt him.
I know your tricks and I'll frustrate your pleasure.
If you were generous and fat with feasting I'd say nothing,
the boy would soon grow fat with you
and feed on your affection;
but keep your hands away from him, or I shall fall upon
you first,
attack your precious members
until you have no strength to urge
your lecherous desires.

THIS graceful fellow Suffenus (you know him well, my
      Varus)
he's witty. He's amusing and writes more verse than anyone.
He must have written out (we'll say) ten thousand poems,
not as we write our stanzas on little scraps of paper,
but on magnificent vellum bound in parchment
with neat red ribbons, rolled securely
in a fine book. But when you read this dainty Suffenus,
the æsthete, a poor illiterate,
a boy who leads a goat or
digs in mud. Go, look at him. Describe him, he's absurd.
This wit, this glittering master
of words at dinner tables, is a poor country boy
or worse at writing poems.
Yet he is never happy, but when creative moods come over
      him and he's
lost in clouds, then he's a god again.
And we (all of us) have the same rich glow, the rapture
when writing verse. And there is no one living
who cannot find within him something of Suffenus,
each his hallucination that blinds him,
nor can he nor his sharp eyes discover
the load on his own shoulders.

FURIUS, you've no slaves, no box to hold your money,

for you have no money,

no spiders (and no walls where spiders live) no hearth, nor
        fire—

father, you have, step-mother, whose teeth grown sharp with
        hunger

split stones. O what a cheerful time you have with them—
        your father,

his wooden wife. All's well and it's no wonder:

you still digest what food may come your way: no falling

house to fear (no home) to be destroyed by fire, wind, or
        rain, or

thieves, no poison will end your lives. Ill fortune
        cannot perfect your ruin.

Your bodies now are dry as old bones, and more so, if it's
        likely

one can be; heat of sun and winter's cold, starvation

will help you. Why here's prosperity!

You cannot sweat, saliva

shall not drip from your lips, you have no phlegm and there-
        fore

no running nose. You're clean; your buttocks are

as clean and pure as salt is;

your bowels refuse to move more than ten times a year and

whatever you discharge is dry and sanitary.
Why beg the gods for more, my Furius, remember
one hundred coins (pure gold) are nothing—
when you're happy.

2 4

YOU are the flower of all the Juventii,
not only in our time but the past and future;
give all the wealth of Midas to that poor dog
who wanders these streets with neither gold nor
    servants—
why do you fasten on him for a lover?
What is he? A prince? And you say "Yes." He is,
    then;
the gentleman with neither gold nor servants!
Ignore me. But I say remember this, remember
he has no slaves to serve him and no money.

2 5

SWEET girlish Thallus, as soft to your caresses as a little
    Spanish rabbit,
delicate as down plucked from a goose, and languid as the
    fallen member
that decorates an old man—but O, a hungry Thallus, covet-
    ous, rapacious,
eager as roaring waves or sea gulls with their beaks wide
    for food—O give me
back my cloak, my Spanish napkins, my ancient Bithynian
    tablets, that you are now displaying—
fool—to show these things in public as yours alone! Drop
    them, your fingers
thick with glue to capture all things. I'll sear you,
your dainty little hips, your pretty hands, and I'll use
whips, inscribing phallus upon your flesh, O Thallus, broken,
    swaying,
lost in a violent storm,—little boat careering through a dark,
    angry ocean.

26

FURIUS, my small estate, my charming villa,
shall never be swept away by the south wind,
nor the west wind, nor the raging north,
nor the little breeze from Asia, but, O, a mortgage,
nfteen thousand, two hundred pieces of gold, here is
    a blast,
a storm that carries ruin and the plague.

2 7

COME, my boy, bring me the best
of good old Falernian:
we must drink down stronger wine
to drink with this mad lady.
Postumia's our host tonight;
drunker than the grape is,
is she—
and no more water;
water is the death of wine.
Serve the stuff to solemn fools
who enjoy their sorrow,
respectable, no doubt—

                  but wine!

Here's wine!

           The very blood of Bacchus!

2 8

FROM Piso's army, bankrupt, your equipment
very light indeed (my Fabullus and best of
good fellows, dear Veranius)
you've served this keg of flat wine,
this monster whose wages are starvation,
paid with winter's cold. How are your books, your
    ledgers;
profits small? (like mine, under my general,
what pay! These were expenses I collected)
O Mummius how you fouled me,
how you pierced me from behind with
the full length of a long pole. My friends,
you look as though you've been served in a like
    manner.
Now, no more dancing after aristocrats, no further
    traffic
with fine families like the Memmii.
May gods bring down quick ruin
upon these swine whose names are
slime on the noble heritage of Romulus and Remus.

WHO can stand by and witness this,
this foul and deep corruption?
If he is silent, he himself is lewd, a drunken swindler.
Mamurra has stripped Gaul and distant Britain
of their wealth. O delicate and girlish
Romulus (O Rome) you love this man? Say nothing?
Then you are like him. He's victorious,
sleeping with every wife in Rome, a shining
white dove or an Adonis.
You witness this, O Romulus,
then you too will sleep with whores,
drink till you fall, and gamble.
And is this why, O conqueror (the one great general of
    Rome)
you captured the remotest
island of the West? To feed this lecherous, impotent
friend of yours, Mamurra, see him spend, scattering
twenty, or thirty millions. Here's disastrous
generosity gone mad. He's already bloated
with banquets and his vices.
His inheritance, his fine estates are shattered:
these were the first to go, then the loot of Pontus
then the wealth of Spain, hear the river Tagus tell the story.
The Gauls and Britons fear him? And you love the monster?

Both of you, Caesar, Pompey? While the beast does nothing,
feeds on wealth and glory. For this, O father-in-law
and son, the world has fallen to ruin.

3 0

ALFENUS, you've betrayed the love of your loyal
      friends and
now turned to stone, no longer see the misery
of him your dearest friend. And there's no wavering
in your mind? Is treachery all you have to give me?
O false as deepest hell. Do the gods reward men
who betray their fellows? And you, you leave me naked
to evil times.
   . . . .
   . . . .
What can men do, in whom shall they discover
new faith? For certainly you held my very soul, I fol-
      lowed,
you led. I thought my love secure, and you, my enemy,
vanish, your words dissolving in air, your promises,
devoured by four winds. No doubt you have forgotten
all you have done and said. But the gods remember
that faith, inevitable, returns, will follow you
forever piercing your brain with grief.

3 1

O MY little almost island, little island Sirmio,

this brave eye, this green-bright jewel set in Neptune's fair
estate

of lucid waters and broad seas.

And it's good to look upon you; even now I can't believe

that the plains lie far behind me, weary Thrace and Bithynia.

You are still secure my own.

After many months of travel, nothing's better than to rest

relaxed and careless; sleep is heaven in our own beloved bed.

Here's enough reward for exile, and long roads through
foreign lands;

now, my Sirmio, greet your master, make these waves bring
laughter up

till the Lydian lakes re-echo all the laughter in my home.

3 2

O MELLOW, sweet, delicious little
piece, my Ipsithilla,
I love you dearly.
Tell me to come at noon
and I'll come galloping
at your threshold.
Let no one bar the door today
but stay at home, my little one,
to fit yourself for nine long
bouts of love. And if you're so inclined,
call me at once;
my morning meal is over
and I reclining
discover
my tree of life (your bedfellow)
has risen joyfully tearing through my clothes,
impatient to be at you.

O MOST successful in the art of stealing clothes
in bath houses is this Vibennius and his lecherous son:
the father skillful in his tricks of sleight of hand
and the son with his rare talent in his buttocks.
And with these gifts the pair should go to hell,
look for another climate;
for the father's tricks are known all over town,
and the son—where can you find a place to sell
your hairy buttocks itching with desire?

XXXIV

DIANAE sumus in fide
puellae et pueri integri:
Dianam pueri integri
puellaeque canamus.

o Latonia, maximi
magna progenies Iouis,
quam mater prope Deliam
deposiuit oliuam,

montium domina ut fores
siluarumque uirentium
saltuumque reconditorum
amniumque sonantum:

tu Lucina dolentibus
Iuno dicta puerperis,
tu potens Triuia et notho's
dicta lumine Luna.

tu cursu, dea, menstruo
metiens iter annuum,
rustica agricolae bonis
tecta frugibus exples.

sis quocumque tibi placet
sancta nomine, Romulique
antique ut solita's bona
sospites ope gentem.

BOYS and girls, we pledge allegiance
to the moon, virgin Diana,
chastity and innocence,
boys and girls all sing Diana.

O divinity, divinest
fruit of Jove, all-powerful sire,
and his Latona, your mother,
gave you birth beneath the sacred

olive tree of Delos, made you
(sing Diana) mistress of the hills,
young forests, hidden valleys
where far winding rivers
disappear in music, sing Diana.

Women in childbirth call upon your name
night goddess, queen of darkness
and false daylight. Sing Diana

who has steered the circling voyage
of the seasons into years,
bringing with her harvest time
and full granaries and rich farms:

by whatever name we call you,
(sing Diana) hear our prayers,

as years long gone you sheltered us
your sons of Romulus from harm
defend, now and forever, sing Diana!

3 5

COME poem, tell my friend,
dear Caecilius, the poet
who writes of love's sweet laughter,
to visit my Verona. Tell him
to leave the city and the shores of Larius.
I have a secret for him, told me by one who
     loves him:
and if his mind is clear, he'll
dissolve the miles between us,
all speed, to greet my words:
if his bright girl, all fire,
embraces him a thousand
times and if she holds him,
pleads him with lips and arms never to leave
     her, then he
must hear me now.

This girl would die for him,
for since she saw the first lines
of what he wrote, his poem in praise of Cybele,
poor dear, she's been distracted,
her body a rich liquid
fire that feeds on love.
I know your passion, dear girl,

whose learned mind re-echoes
sweetest of Sapphic metres,
for Caecilius has shown her
his song to the "Great Mother."

3 6

ANNALS of Volusius. O what toilet paper!
Anyway you'll make my girl keep her word to Venus—
Venus and her cupids—she swore if I stopped writing
my bitter foul iambics and made love to her again
she'd give fuel to lame Vulcan,
Poetry, the most delectable of all bad poetry written
to the glowing ashes of a cursed, blasted tree.
She saw at once this treasure,
superlative of all that's bad to serve the merry gods for
an evening of rare laughter.
Therefore I say, O Venus,
sprung from divine blue oceans,
who walks through holy Cyprus, who travels wind-swept
    Urii,
who lives in her Ancona, within her sacred temple,
or where reeds grow in Cnidus, in Amathus, in Golgi,
or in Dyrrachium, the seaport where men gather
from all of Sicily.
Now note that my girl's promise
is kept, an offering since it's not unbecoming
serves well. Down to the flames with
this amateurish drivel.
Annals of Volusius. O what toilet paper!

Roadhouse and members of that bawdy fraternity
that roars behind the ninth pillar
from the temple where those two brothers, Castor and Pollux
wear their caps, signifying good fortune. Are you the only
men on earth fit to mount girls and ride them, the rest of us,
merely goats?
Come now, line up,
bent double in a circle, a hundred of you, or two hundred,
come, do you think I am not able to take on
two hundred of you in one grand bout of pederasty?
What's more I'll cover the front doors of your fine house
with nimble sketches of the phallus.
My girl has left me,
loved more than any woman born was she,
and I have fought, spilled blood for her,
but she has taken this house for a place to sleep and live.
O great and noble gentlemen, she's slept with all of you
to her dishonour, slept with pimps
that walk at night in darkest alley-ways,
and you, particularly, dainty, long-haired Egnatius,
son of a homosexual Spanish rabbit,
made handsome by an ancient Spanish custom,
your beard and teeth daily and delicately
bathed in Spanish urine.

38

MY friend Cornificus, your friend Catullus
is a sick man indeed, growing worse every day, every hour.
What have you done for him—said a word to cure his ill-
ness?
and a word costs nothing!
Send me a line; say something, something that will ease me
now,
or send me a tear, sad as the sorrow of that tender fellow
poet, Simonides.

EGNATIUS has white teeth and therefore always pleasant,
    always smiling;
and if a lawyer is telling a sad tale for the defense (a pitiful
    client),
Egnatius is there with his eternal smile.
If there's a funeral with the mother weeping
over the body of her only son,
Egnatius arrives gleaming with his happy smile:
no matter where he is or who he sees or what he does,
he is forever smiling.
                O what a foul disease,
this smile,
          not sweet nor gracious,
nor a sign of social charm.
                    Listen to me, my dear,
good, fine Egnatius,
                if you were Roman, Sabine, Tibertine,
or a starved greedy pig from Umbria,
or an Etruscan, short and round, or a dark Lanuvian
with glittering teeth or a man from my own province,
or anybody at all who scrubs his teeth with good clean water
    daily—
your smile would still offend me; nothing is worse
than senseless laughter from a foolish face. But you're a
    Spaniard,

and we already know the Spanish custom:

how Spaniards clean their teeth
and scour their gums with the same water that issues
from their bladders.

So if your teeth are clean, my friend, we know how
you have used your urine.

40

WHAT feeble-minded mood, poor crazy Ravidus,
directed you and set you in the way of all
my terrible iambics?
What god has steered you
into this lost cause, this brainless warfare?
Come, was it then the hope
of notoriety, of gossip—or anything for fame,
or infamy,
for if you must go, go, love this boy
and be my rival, take your punishment,
that's sure to follow you
many long years.

41

SEE that girl, Ameana, the one with the big nostrils?
She's the little parasite of that wild boy, Mamurra
and the girl is suing me for a full ten thousand—
personal services of course—
someone tell her father,
mother, sister, aunt, or friends to call in a physician,
have him work upon her brain. The poor creature's crazy.
But don't blame me or ask me why or where or how.
A looking-glass must strike her blind—
O what a face and what hallucinations!

42

COME to me, my poems, all my far-flung armies
marching out in time with eleven bitter syllables,
some filthy, naked whore has seized upon my papers,
walked away with them and now she won't return them.
Hound her down, my boys—and who is she?

         I'll tell you:
she's that female beast that walks about the streets here
proud of herself and bold (not even with the grace of
a human animal) laughing with her tongue out
like a Gallic bitch.

     O my boys, surround her,
chant your claim against her:

    "Dirty little bitch,
     give us back our poems,
     give us back our poems."
What? She doesn't hear? Then louder:
    "Lousy bloody whore,
     bitch littered in a
     brothel——"
but even these sweet names can never make you blush now
(blushing never was a special trait of bitches);
still she's quite unmoved, and we must change our tactics,
say to her:

    "O beautiful sweet untarnished virgin."
56

43

LISTEN, girl: your nose is not too small and
your foot somehow lacks shapeliness, your eyes
are not so bright, your fingers though they should be
are neither long nor graceful, nor can your lips
(mouth dripping) be kissed for love, nor is your speech
soft music.
And this girl is the lady friend
of that debauched citizen Mamurra.
They say that you are lovely (rumours from
    the provinces)
comparing you with Lesbia.

The times are bad
and this an ignorant generation.

44

O MY estate, my farm, Tivolian or Sabine,
(and those who would not break my heart say that I live in
    Tivoli,
correct and fashionable while others swear that my estate
is merely crude and Sabine)
however, both will do, Tivolian or Sabine.
At least, you shelter me in a suburban home,
a place for willing exile to cure this dreadful cold within
    my chest, well-earned
through heavy meals. My stomach's far too busy,
too eager for rich banquets.

While I was on my way
to feast with Sestius, I read his pamphlet on
the candidate Antius dripping with pus and bile, contagious
    stuff.
At once I caught a chill, coughed,
then fell apart with sickness.
Diseased I hurried home
to you, my farm, lay curled between your breasts,
slept and restored my health on vegetable diet.
Now that I'm well again,
I'll thank my home, my villa, for saving me the just rewards
    of dissipation.

And now, if ever again I read my friend Sestius,
before he takes me dining, I'll see to it that he, not I,
after a violent book is read, falls sick abed
with chills and fever.

SEPTIMIUS with his arms entwined round his Acme
says: my dear, if I do not love to destruction
down the long road to hell and love but you forever,
may I wander lonely through India, Africa,
and be discovered, naked, by a green-eyed, ravenous lion.

As he spoke, Love sneezed, an omen of good fortune.

Then Acme, head thrown back, her eyes, her fluid body
drunken with love, her rose-red lips to his replying:
here's my life, Septimius. I swear to serve my lord till
flames of love consume me, now flowing through my veins and
melting me. The core of my being turns to fire.

Love sneezed again and they received his own, his sacred
        blessing.
Under his wings, they marched forth, love for love, united,
blood fused in a rich liquid.

Septimius, a poor young man, finds more wealth in his Acme
than all the gold of Britain and the mines of Syria.
He is her life. His arms alone hold pleasure for sweet Acme.
Is there good fortune on this earth equal to his treasure;
who shall see again and know greater love than theirs is?

46

NOW warm-smelling Spring has come
and here's our sweet weather,
and the gallant West wind
clears dark April skies.
Say good-bye, Catullus, to the plains of Asia Minor,
leave these spawning farmlands
and heat-sick Nicaea.
We shall sail, shall fly
to our fair Aegean cities.
Now my soul grows swift wings, look, my feet are dancing,
they shall lead the way.
O my friends, good-bye,
good-bye my fellow exiles, many miles from Italy,
for our ways dissever,
each to his own pleasure,
each to his own home.

SOCRATION and Porcius,
two scrofulous
right hands of Consul Piso,
synonymous with greed and plague
devouring our country. The great god Priapus,
erect, has served your pleasure:
look, a banquet spread at noon,
you feed and spawn,
drunken in the sunlight.
And my friends, dear Fabullus
and my little Veranius, starve, forever walking
down city streets to find a meal,
gazing at banquets, wondering who
will take them in for dinner.

48

O IF you would let me, fair Juventius,
I would be kissing your honeyed eyes forever.
Three hundred thousand times I would kiss you
with new rapture,
nor could find enough of this blissful pastime
promised in my dreams. Even if our kisses
grew to such profusion
they outnumbered sheaves
ripening in the wheat field.

OF all the sons of Romulus who walk the earth,
giants of the past or those who follow us,
your eloquence, Citizen Marcus Tullius,
rises above all others. Here, Catullus
offers you his deepest gratitude,
and he is by far the humblest poet of his kind,
as you are great, O Cicero!
in your exalted honourable profession.

50

YESTERDAY was a feast Licinius,
a round of poetry, my poems read aloud,
and then we joined in making
many a neat love song, each in his turn
writing a new stanza, O Licinius,
we galloped with new metres, laughter and wine
ran through us, your genius set
my blood on fire.
And now at home, I cannot sleep,
eyes staring round, awake, my legs and arms
alive between the sheets,
waiting for morning and another word from you,
until exhausted, I am all but dead.
I make this poem for you, read it, friend;
see (O what torture!) you have done to me.
Now read these lines with care, light of my eyes
or Nemesis shall haunt you night and day;
This goddess won't forgive you, nor forget
your crimes if you ignore
my poem.

51

HE is changed to a god he who looks on her,
godlike he shines when he's seated beside her,
immortal joy to gaze and hear the fall of
        her sweet laughter.

All of my senses are lost and confounded;
Lesbia rises before me and trembling
I sink into earth and swift dissolution
        seizes my body.

Limbs are pierced with fire and the heavy tongue fails,
ears resound with noise of distant storms shaking
this earth, eyes gaze on stars that fall forever
        into deep midnight.

*   *   *   *   *   *

This languid madness destroys you Catullus,
long day and night shall be desolate, broken,
as long ago ancient kings and rich cities
        fell into ruin.

*   *   *   *   *   *

52

WHAT is this, Catullus? Why not prepare your funeral?
For Nonius, a foul disease, is seated in high office.
Look at this scrofulous tumor, while this Vatinius
pays homage to his power.
Why not die, Catullus?

53

WHILE my dear friend Calvus was exposing all the crimes of
Vatinius in the Forum, I laughed aloud, I shouted
to see someone throw his hands up and roar with admiration:
"Gods on earth, what eloquence
from this talking pigmy!"

5 4

OTHO'S brains are small—look at his head.

    *   *   *   *   *

Your dirty legs are like a slave's.

    *   *   *   *   *

I would enjoy your hatred, Libonis, O aged,
the delicate homosexual, and you Fuficius
whose vital members bloom
with eternal fire.

    *   *   *   *   *

You and everyone will cry out against
my terrible iambics.

WHERE'S your dark cave, Camerius,
come tell me where you're hiding.
Here's no intrusion, friend, I merely want to know where
you are. For I've inquired
throughout the little Campus,
the bookstores and Jove's temple
and even Pompey's theatre.
Camerius had vanished but girls with sweet blank faces
    looked into mine:
O little whores, where is he
dear Camerius? A little girl, half naked,
showed me her breasts, said: here he's
asleep between my roses.
The struggles and the torments of Hercules are nothing
to this search for you, my friend . . .
O if I were the guardian of Crete, the great bronze Talus,
or Ladas, the swift Spartan, or flying Pegasus,
or winged Perseus or the thundering horses
Ulysses stole from Rhesus,
my search would still be useless;
though all these gods and creatures were made to fit my
    service
in finding you, Camerius, I'd be worn out, defeated . . .
Why so remote, my dearest friend, bring sunshine to dark
    places.

Is there a girl, a milk-fed girl who hides you in her bosom?

Your tongue is lost within your mouth—but Venus takes
no pleasure

in speechless friends and lovers. Still silent? Then I leave
you

content if you will let me own

one share in your affections.

O CATO listen, here's something so fantastic
it deserves your laughter,
laugh then as heartily as you love your Catullus:

I saw a boy and girl (the boy on top) so I fell,
chiefly to please Dione,
upon the boy and pierced him,
held him to his duty with my rigid spearhead.

WHAT a pair of pretty boys, Caesar and Mamurra,
both decadent with secret lust,
nor is it any wonder
both tainted by the sewers of Formiae and the city,
sick with the same diseases.
See the loving twins abed,
graced with the same learning and the same quick
    appetite
for wives of other men. O see them conquering every
    girl
in sight and still they're hungry,
what a pair of pretty boys, Caesar and Mamurra.

58

CAELIUS, my Lesbia, that one, that only Lesbia,
Lesbia whom Catullus loved more than himself and all
    things
he ever owned or treasured.
Now her body's given up in alley-ways,
on highroads to these fine Roman gentlemen,
fathered centuries ago by the noble Remus.

59

RUFA from Bologna, wife of Menenius,
spends her time abed
draining the strength of Rufulus.
You must have seen the creature
at a funeral pyre, stealing food that's baking
with the bodies of the dead.
You remember how she seized a loaf of bread and
how a dirty slave drove her (O, what a beating)
from his master's graveyard.

60

WERE you born of a lioness in the Libyan Mountains,
or that half-woman monster, Scylla,
screaming in the lowest chambers of her womb,
sent forth already merciless and hard,
one who could never hear the cries of a man, even in his
  mortal agony,
O heart made bitter and cruel beyond all measure.

61

ON that hill (O Helicon
where the muses gather)
there the son of all the vast planetary systems
walks in eternal splendour
giving blossoming girls away
to young men striding homeward,
O Hymenaee, Hymen,
O Hymen, Hymenaee.

Wreath the sweet marjoram
blooming through the shadows
of the golden wedding veil round round your head,
  O virgin,
come to us revealing (in fatal
golden slippers) feet
more beautiful than snow
fallen in the sunlight.

Wake upon this holiday
radiating music
of bells against the morning sky;
quick feet shake the ground and
the fiery pine torch sways in hands that chime the
   measure
of the marriage dance.

O bride,
join our celebration.

Vinia who shines as fair
as the fair young Venus
the very girl that Paris saw rising out of Cyprus,
is this chaste bride (with birds in flight above her)
marrying our Manlius and
bringing us good fortune,
and the girl is sweeter far
than white-blossomed myrtle
flowering out of Asia, springing from wild gardens
where the Hamadryads give
birth to trees and flowers.

Come, you nymphs and leave behind
caves and cliffs and valleys
round the grassy pregnant hill (O Helicon, eternal,
where sweet rain forever pours
from Aganippe's fountain)
then bring our virgin home
to her husband's threshold,
graced with a girlish love that is half-modest and
    half-eager
now, O nymphs entwine her heart
with love in the same fashion
that ivy covers a tall tree
growing in ancient gardens.

78

Follow me, immaculate,
(O most perfect virgins)
you shall have a day like this soon; come, sing in
    measure:
O Hymenaee, Hymen,
O Hymen, Hymenaee.

What god deserves more passion from
passion-inspired lovers
than you,
and hearing this, the mighty god
shall rise again, triumphant,
performing holy ritual, assisting our chaste Venus
who pours a benediction on
the marriage of true lovers.

What god deserves more passion from
passion-inspired lovers
than you, and of all gods on high
who should receive full tribute
from every man and every girl
within his vast dominions?
O Hymenaee, Hymen,
O Hymen, Hymenaee.

Palsied, frail old men bow down
to you in supplication, offering you their daughters

and young girls, no longer fearful,
come naked, walk before you, singing praise,
    almighty god,
see the trembling bridegroom,
blood on fire to hear your answer.

You give the flowering bride away,
(warm from her mother's shelter)
into the powerful encircling arms
of a flaming bridegroom:
O Hymenaee, Hymen,
O Hymen, Hymenaee.

Without your holy ritual
Venus herself could never
meet the just approval of the virtuous household
where is the god who is mightier than you are?

Even great Venus herself
bows before you
(she has no honour in any virtuous household
failing your sacrament,
enduring beyond her)
where is the god who is mightier than you are?

Where is the land
that could breed men without you;
you with your power

over birth and conception.
Where is the god who is mightier than you are?

Where is the king
who could breed iron armies
marching in legions against an invader
without your consent in the holy
vows of marriage.
Where is the god who is mightier than you are?

Locks are sprung apart
and the gates are slowly opened;
now the moment comes for the virgin to appear.
See the marriage torches shake
their golden hair upon us?

    * * * * * * *
    * * * * * * *
    * * * * * * *
    * * * * * * *

Gently nurtured maidens
are slow with their advances,
(afraid of her own passion
so she is lingering, fearing her desires
rising with small breasts)
this ritual too long:
hearing this, she weeps and she cannot still
her weeping.

Come, no more tears my girl,
for nothing here shall harm you;
you are more fair (O Vinia) than any
girl on earth who saw this morning's sun rise
out of Eastern Oceans.

You, the blue-eyed larkspur
growing in the garden of
a lord's estate—but still you are not coming.
Come then with this hour,
for the day speeds onward.

Come then with this hour
for the flaming torches
shake their golden heads, scattering gold upon us
when they hear us singing:
come then with this hour.

And the man who marries you
knows that he will never
make your bed adulterous but will sleep forever
with his head between your breasts
your limbs his limbs entwining
as the flexible nervous vine winds about a tree and
mingles with its branches.
Come then with this hour,
for the day speeds onward.

To the marriage bed and all . . .

* * * * * * *

* * * * * * *

* * * * * * *

O ivory-footed bedstead.

O what pleasures wait for him
who shall be your master
under the swift wings of night,
what miraculous rapture
wakens when the light of day uncovers his pos-
    sessions.
Come then with this hour
for the day speeds onward.

Swing your torches overhead
boys, the glittering veil
of the bride's in sight
make her blushing beauty rise
with your glorious noises:
O Hymen, Hymenaee,
hail O Hymen, Hymenaee.

We shall make another song
to sing in streets and alleys:
let this pretty boy who's now
forsaken by his master give sweet nuts to let us
    know

he's no longer mistress
of our bridegroom's tender heart
and his fragrant body.

You've been pampered long enough
sweet boy, serve in the household
of a man who takes a wife in the old tradition
of the rugged warrior
who plucked a Sabine beauty.

It was only yesterday
you snubbed the honest wives of
foremen on your master's farms, now your boyish
    charms are
fallen. And your hour is done,
lovely pitiful creature.

Thrust your pretty boys aside
(sweet-smelling bridegroom) lovers
must vanish in the image of
your own marriage chamber.
O Hymen, Hymenaee,
Hail O Hymen Hymenaee.

We who know you know that all
your lovers will be forgotten;
that your yesterdays are dead with all their childish
    pleasures.

O Hymen, Hymenaee,
Hail O Hymen Hymenaee.

Never O bride, use your fair limbs
to breed frustrated passion
in your husband's bed, give him his desire.
O Hymen, Hymenaee
Hail O Hymen Hymenaee.

Worship this rich virility
who by this act endows you
with the increasing glory of his name and house,
serve him in mind and body
(O Hymen, Hymenaee,
Hail O Hymen Hymenaee)

till you are old, and head and limbs
trembling, forever saying yes
to your lord and master.
O Hymen, Hymenaee,
Hail O Hymen Hymenaee.

Stride with careful step across
the threshold where good fortune
follows golden feet that vanish, never faltering,
within the radiant doorway.
O Hymen, Hymenaee,
Hail O Hymen Hymenaee.

See the crimson marriage bed
where your fair young husband
burns (all eagerness) intent upon your beauty.
O Hymen, Hymenaee
Hail O Hymen Hymenaee.

No less than yours his love is great
but the flames are hidden
in a secret place (O bride) that you alone discover.
O Hymen, Hymenaee,
Hail O Hymen Hymenaee.

Tell the boy (that little child
dressed in cloth of purple)
to release the bride's right arm, let her meet her
    husband.
O Hymen, Hymenaee,
Hail O Hymen Hymenaee.

Tell the honoured guests to rise,
man and wife together;
they must put the bride to bed, for her husband's
    ready.
O Hymen, Hymenaee,
Hail O Hymen Hymenaee.

Now, young man, your bride's abed
to be made a wife. O

see her flowering among poppies and sweet asters.
You are handsome as she is
beautiful (O Venus
made this pair for love)—but the day speeds
    onward.
Let the young man make the girl
his wife now and forever
with the help of Venus
who presides omnipotent at this solemn union.
You have done your marriage vow,
we have seen your pleasure
in the full round light of day (let them count the
    number
of the stars set in the sky,
let them count the grains of
sand that covers Africa,
those who care to measure all the raptures you
    have found
in your first communion).
Let this glorious pair conceive
a child before tomorrow's sun has risen
to propagate a hallowed name, forever piercing
the dark clouds of the future;
grant me sight to see small Manlius
turn from his mother's breasts and
stare, smiling at his father.

May the boy grow handsomely,
like in every feature
to the man who gave him birth,
proof to every stranger that here is Manlius come
    to earth
again, the boy a symbol
of the immortal virtue rising from his mother's
    womb.
May this boy convert her worth
to deeds and so inherit
the strength that chaste Penelope gave to her son,
    his name
resounding her fame and his forever.

Come virgins, for the day is done
we've no more song to give them.
The doors are closed. Husband and wife are joined.
Their youthful love will breed
a vigorous generation.

BOYS

TWILIGHT and star we hope to see arise, pouring bright rain
  from Mount Olympus down
over the wedding feast, have now arrived, we sing our praise
  to the advancing bride,
rise now to greet her singing:
O Hymen, Hymenaee, come now, O Hymen.

GIRLS

And is it true that Hesperus is here? Witness this company of
  boys now standing
facing us and the star of night flames with the fire of Mount
  Oeta,
O hear them sing and see their ritual, wonder and joy for us
  to gaze upon
O Hymen, Hymenaee, come now, O Hymen.

BOYS

Hear how the girls have set their song in perfect measures,
  and each word recited
sounds from an infallible memory, surely their minds were
  rooted
deep in memorable music while we (our minds and ears distracted) wandered, and we shall be outdone;
O victory shall fall to those who sing in perfect rhythm, we

must equal them and what they say must find
our words a perfect compliment.
O Hymen, Hymenaee, come now, O Hymen.

What are these flames that roll against the skies, divorcing
    mother and child, more terrible
than earthly fires? These flames of Hesperus that seize a
    daughter from her mother's arms
delivering the girl into the quick embrace of a young hus-
    band—here is destruction greater
than a tall city given to its enemies.
O Hymen, Hymenaee, come now, O Hymen.

BOYS

What is more beautiful than this rich fire, the crown of
    heaven rising,
the fire that joins the marriage a true contract spoken by
    husband and parents of the bride,
and yet does not disclose its vital power until the marriage
    bed is made. What a gift from heaven
greater than this gift from gods to man in a superlative hour
    of happiness?
O Hymen, Hymenaee, come now, O Hymen.

* * * * * * * *

GIRLS

O friends who love us, Hesperus has taken one of us, our sister, taken. . . .

* * * * * * *

BOYS

O Hesperus when you rise, our guardian, eyes open the night
    long,
you come, disguised as dawn star now disclosing thieves hid-
    den under night's vast shadow
but virgins cry against you, a false lamentation against him
    who is desire
coiled in their brains, a secret never spoken.
O Hymen, Hymenaee, come now, O Hymen.

GIRLS

We are as flowers in a garden hidden from all men's eyes, no
    creature of the field walks in this place,
no plow divides us; only the gentlest wind, rain from a soft
    warm cloud and the quickening sun to nourish us.
We are the treasure that many girls and boys desire; but once
    deflowered (the flower stained and torn)
the virgin's body rancid, neither boys nor girls will turn to
    her again
nor can she wake their passion.

You are as a vine in a barren field that cannot climb by its
   own strength

nor its fruit prosper (the vine driven downward with its own
   weight neither the ox nor plowman shall teach it how

to grow, but if its body twined round an elm, gives promise of
   fruit, then by this marriage

many a farmer and his beast will wait upon it). So is it
   with you O virgins.

The virgin, perfect, wastes until she ripens in the marriage
   bed and there receives

her father's blessing and her husband's love.

Never resist the power of this union made, O virgin; father
   and mother have given you to him, this man, your
   husband

your maidenhead by this division is not yours alone, you hold
   one third of that which is the treasure

of parents and your husband—this is the lawful contract
   given to him whose hands.receive your dowry.

O Hymen, Hymenaee, come now, O Hymen.

ATTIS propelled by his swift ship through deep waves, set
    his quick feet upon the Phrygian shore;
entered the heavy sunless forest where his mind grew dark as
    shadows over him
and there, his blood gone mad, seized a sharp stone, divorced
    his vital members from his body,
then rising (the ground wet with blood) he was transformed,
    a woman with her delicate white hands
sounding the tympanum, the tympanum singing praise
    through sacred trumpets raised to goddess Cybele,
mysterious mother of a sexless race.
Then in his sweet falsetto Attis sang: Now follow me, O
    priests of Cybele, come follow, we are creatures
of this goddess, wind, dance, unwind the dance again, O exiles
    from a far land, come with me
across the rapid salt sea wave. Your bodies shall be clean; no
    more shall Venus
stain you with foul disease and move your limbs with power
    of love.
Now under my leadership (this mad delight) land in her rich
    dominions, sing you her praise
make her heart leap with the same joy that rises in your blood
    at this sweet liberty.
No longer wait for her, but come, follow my way that winds
    upward to her temple,

making glad noises with the pipe that plays a song to welcome her,
clash cymbals, dance and shake the earth with thunder, your
  quick feet sounding her glory, and like the girls
who follow Bacchus, toss your heads, shout songs in measure
  to the Phrygian pipes, come join her merry
company where drunken cries rise in a chorus. The sacred
  symbol of her worship trembles in air
that moves with noise poured from your lips here in this
  place where the great goddess wanders.

Now Attis (not quite woman) called her followers, leading
  then toward green blooming Ida where
his followers crowded, tongues trembling with shrill noises,
  hollow cymbals crashed and the tympanum rang again,
  again
the race sped forward. Then wavering exhausted, the ghost of
  their very lives issuing
from lips, circling in delirium they followed Attis through
  the green shadows, she who sprang
like a raging heifer freed from harness, till they sank, defeated (weariness in their eyes, and starved for lack
  of food) at the high temple of Cybele, their goddess,
then madness declined into a heavy wave of sleep, minds
  sunk in darkness.

But when the sun transformed the skies into a radiant heaven,
> his mighty rolling brilliant eye

disclosing hills, the savage sea all in clear outlines, and there
> was liquid peace within his mind, the horses

of dawn rose galloping, trampling night underfoot, and
> Attis, leaving sweet Pasithea wife of sleep, awoke,

looked back and saw what he had done, how his mad brain
> deceived him saw how he lost

his manhood—all this in passionless clarity seized his mind,
> and with his eyes turned homeward

across the sea, she wept, poor creature, neither man nor
> woman.

Land of my birth, creating me, my fatherland I left you (O
> miserably, a fugitive)

I have gone into this wilderness of snow to live with beasts
> that circle Ida's mountain,

my brain in darkness—and where are you, land of my
> fathers, for you have vanished and my eyes return

where you once rose before me. In this short hour while my
> brain still welcomes sunlight,

I praise you—now shall I be driven back into this wilderness
> where everyone,

my friends, my parents, and all I love shall fade. I shall not
> walk again through the city streets, nor join the crowd,

(O glorious young men) who fill the stadium and who excel
> in many pleasures.

Look at my misery and hear me cry my curse against this
   miserable fate,
I am a woman, hear my voice and look at me who once walked
   bravely hero of games, a boy who stood
rich flower of youth equal to all who challenged him. All
   these were mine: friends crowding at my door,
wreaths of sweet flowers in my room when morning sun
   called me away, and a welcome threshold that I left
behind me. Witness me, a girl, a slave of Cybele, dressed like
   a girlish follower of Bacchus,
half my soul destroyed, and sterile I must live on this cold
   mountain
and like all others in snow-bound Ida's province, follow the
   deer and wild boar—a man undone,
longing for home again. And as these words flowed from her
   glowing lips a prayer rose to the gods,
Cybele released her lions, driving one nearest to her side into
   the forest saying:

Go follow him, he who is mad Attis, mangle his brain within
   your claws, go follow
him who longs to leave my empire; give your rage to him,
   transmute your madness to his person,
lash tail and throw your rolling head, mane erect in fury,
   follow him.

96

At this the creature sprang through the deep wilderness, and
   on a glittering sunstruck beach found Attis
drove him back to Ida where now wandering forever Attis
   delirious, sings praise, a servant to the goddess Cybele.

Great goddess, spare me, never haunt my home—take others
   for your slaves, those creatures
that you have driven mad and those who in their madness
   wake again your passionate cruelty.

FROM Pelion these ancient trees transfigured (so they tell
 us) into ships, pierced the waters,
of Neptune's kingdom, entering the river Phasis, came to
 rest upon the shores
where king Æetes rules the land. O Argonauts. The magnificent youth of Greece
speeding through salt waves breaking on foreign shores to
 gain the Golden Fleece, their swift oars bearing
this sea chariot, fashioned by the goddess guarding towering
 skylines of our cities;
with her delicately powerful hands she wove the keel of this
 ship steering
by frail winds from a calm sky, she who taught uncharted
 sea waves how a
ship sails unknown waters.
So was she when her prow broke through windspray and her
 oars spun through foam
where sea nymphs rose, amazed at this swift miracle; then
 sailors saw them, the first sight to mortal eyes
of their red nipples in white foam. At this time (so runs
 the legend) Peleus at one glance glowed
with fire of love for Thetis, nor did Thetis turn her mind
 from mortal flesh in marriage then.

Jupiter, the father, saw that Peleus was born for her bed. O
    golden age when these heroes
sprang from gods, witness my praise! O excellent mothers of
    this breed, here is my tribune and may songs
recite your worth now and forever, bringing you to life
    again—
most of all, these two sweet lovers to be joined in holy
    marriage,
Jupiter almighty, himself, gave his Thetis (once his own)
    to the pillar of Thessaly.
She was yours, O Jupiter, for the mistress of the waters that
    encircle earth had given
you the right to master her, now the bride of Peleus.
When at last the marriage holiday arrives, all Thessaly,
    dressed in splendour, floods the palace, welcoming
bride and bridegroom. Here the guests bear marriage gifts in
    their arms, their faces luminous
with joy. See the empty streets of Cieros, houses left un-
    tenanted, and the valley of Tempe now deserted,
all are gathered to Pharsalus where the marriage feast is
    waiting; fields and meadows lie forgotten,
cattle graze in lonely pastures, vineyards wild, the fruit un-
    ripened, pale and die under the shadows
of tall trees commingling with the vine, the earth no longer
    torn by the downward thrusting

99

ox-drawn share, the plow deserted, turns to rust. But all the
    rich lands
where the home of Peleus rises flower with opulence and the
    hallways
of the palace, radiant with gold and silver, lead the way to
    glittering tables;
sunlight streams from ivory thrones and the light reflected
    flows
over all the treasure gathered; the entire house sways
    drunken with its splendour, echoing
laughter from divine lips breaking. Here encircled by royal
    opulence the marriage bed is waiting
(ivory feet and purple robes, iridescent sea shells shining
    through the draperies) O sea goddess!
On this bed a tapestry weaves the legend of old heroes and
    their deeds. See Ariadna
gazing from the wave resounding shores of Dia, see her
    trembling (heart torn with mad love) as Thetis
sails upon the far horizon. Shaken from dark sleep and
    dreams that betrayed her, Ariadna
gazes stricken, unbelieving at this vision of swift oars bear-
    ing him, the thoughtless lover, gone from her,
his promises now mingled with the roaring sea winds rising
    to the empty skies. She stands deserted
helpless on her lonely shore.

Now as Theseus plunges oarstruck waves, a daughter of Minos
    rises from seaweed (and like Bacchante
carved from marble, mad with tears and oceanic passion in
    her blood all grief now stripped and trembling
stands full naked) girdle fallen from her breasts and delicate
    headdress
in salt waves at her feet. But she, her mind in passion, fixed
    on you O Theseus,
cared nothing for dress, spirit, mind, body lost in darkness
that filled her brain, poor girl (the brain gone mad, hung in
    mid-air terrified)
for Venus poured maddening grief into her heart from the
    very hour that Theseus
aggressive, brave, left the embracing arms of Piræus harbour
    and strode the palace of the Cretan King.

It has been said (in ancient times) how all Cecropia (Athens
    now) was forced by fire and plague to offer up
virgins and boys, atonement for the murder of Androgeos,
    these children fed to the bull, Minotaur.
Theseus had seen the very walls of his own city tremble with
    this curse, offered his body
rather than see these fair young creatures (living yet dead
    and doomed to sail for Crete and the dread monster)
turn into flames that feed a funeral pyre. Then with little
    navy of swift ships leaping the waves with fair winds,

he arrived at the magnificent palace of almighty Minos,
    King of Crete. There the King's daughter
saw him with love's own brilliant eye, she who still dreamed
    of the sweet-smelling breasts where she lay as a child
coiled within the shelter of her mother's body. She turned
    to him, drawn as powerfully
as the quick warmth of spring makes myrtles bloom upon
    the banks of Eurotas and all bright flowers
that rise to April sun. She gazed until the flames within her
    eyes ran downward through her veins
consuming all her body and the core of life within her turned
    to fire.
O god of love! this boy who creates a mixture of misery and
    rapture, a fluid that fills the hearts of men,
who rules forever Golgi and forest-green Idalium! What are
    these storms, these waves where you have thrown
this girl, all flames, breathing in sighs for this unknown man,
    this creature with the golden hair.
See her heart trembling, see how a yellow pallor of fear
    spreads over her as marching Theseus
eager for victory or death, closes his battle with bull
    Minotaur.
And though sweet incense, a frail, wordless prayer issuing,
    rising from her lips did not reach heaven,
the gods were not unknowing, not ungrateful. Theseus was as
    a tree on Mount Taurus swaying,

an oak, or a powerful self-breeding pine, torn by a storm at
     root and falling, mangles
all life under its weight, and in this fashion Theseus con-
     quered the bull, its body crushed lifeless
upon the earth, only the head swayed slowly, horns piercing
     empty winds circling the ground.
Then Theseus returned all glory now, stepping his way with
     infinite care so as not to lose
sight of the thread (given him by Ariadna) trailing the way
     out of the maze surrounding him.

But I must not digress—for Ariadna is the heroine of my
     song, must tell how she had left behind her
the memory of her father's sister, and last her mother now
     fading lost, the symbol of grief
for a daughter who had betrayed Crete all for love of
     Theseus; how the ship rocked at the foam-white shores
     of Dia and
how when her eyes were locked in sleep, her husband van-
     ished, the bridal bed forgotten.
They say that she went mad, her voice a trumpet sound of
     grief, wordless issuing from her heart, her body driven
to climb high mountain tops, eyes staring at empty oceans,
     and then returning wading waist deep, garments floating
in rolling waves. Then she would weep, as a woman in the
     last hour of life, frozen, her face a mask of tears.

So it was you, Theseus, who carried me away from a father's
hearth, to this lonely shore, O hell-born Theseus!
who has forgotten me and the holy commands issued by the
gods, and you shall bear the curse (my curse upon you)
of a memory that fails all promises, even to your own home.
O mind fixed on a single purpose, cruel,
no pity in your heart, merely a sweet voice reciting promises
that fail, that gave me hope when hope was gone.
There was a vision of a blessed marriage, now an empty
wind rising to heaven and from this hour
may no woman believe what men say, for men (minds set
upon a single end) will promise everything,
but once the shrewd mind satisfies its passion, it plunges
forward (the broken promise merely words that trail
behind tall bravery). Remember, Theseus, when you leaned
over the edge of death, almost fallen,
I sacrificed my brother, the bull Minotaur rather than lose
your love, (turned faithless now)
My loyalty to you shall curse my body in death, torn by
beasts and birds of the air, nor find in death a resting
place, not even
a handful of earth over my remains. O were you born of a
lion in a desert cave
or were you conceived and tossed out of an angry ocean,
child of terror and desolation,

arid sands mothered by the twin monsters Scylla and
    Charybdis,
who live only to vomit forth creatures like you from their
    vital organs;
if you feared marriage with me would breed your father's
    anger,
you could have taken me in chains of love
to wash your feet in clear, running waters, tend you at night,
    cover your bed and I would be your slave.
Why should I weep forever into the winds that cannot hear
    me; merely
taking my breath out of my lips and silently wiping my tears
    and all my sorrow
becomes an echo with no voice but my own. This hour is my
    last hour of life; him whom I love is swaying,
rocked by mighty waves beyond the sight of man. Here in
    this wilderness, good fortune led by grief has turned
    to evil
no one shall hear me in this hour of death.

O Jupiter, omnipotent, I would undo time and chance that
    brought the Greek ships to my Cretan shores,
and this wandering faithless lover whose mouth was filled
    with lies, undo the fatal truce
betraying the bull Minotaur, undo the fate that anchored
    this sailor, the spirit of hell disguised as man

in my beloved Crete. I curse his cruelty hidden by soft words.
This man had taken
our palace as his home—but where is my home now, for
Crete is lost forever;
turgid seas divide me from its shores. Where are the hills of
Sidon; they have vanished beyond these waters.
How can I now return to rest, encircled by my father's arms,
I left him for a lover whose hands
are stained with my brother's blood, nor can I find relief in
him who flows over dark waves,
he is the wind—his oars are plunged into the sea, he roars
against the tide.

Here silence and sand cover my words with silence and sand
again, this is my only shelter and hope,
a nightmare with the familiar face of death rising within my
dreams.
But now before death has covered the light of my eyes with
his dark hand, before all that I see, feel, hear has
sunken
into the ground, and there is relief at last even for this body
that knows no rest, only disease of the mind and pain—
I shall call upon the gods, my last words echoing my sobs
resounding against high heaven,
in this my last, my final hour.

Hear me gods whose antiquity flows backward beyond the
        time of man, whose vengeance falls on all, O wake again
with snakes circling your foreheads and now releasing rivers
        of blood pouring from sightless eyes,
make these the signals of the anger (red coals in your
        breasts) that brings you out of the forgotten
womb of time. Hear what I say, look at my heart, wrapped
        round with flames, my soul in madness, O remember
these last words spoken from my heart, O gods! And as
        Theseus has now forgotten me, make him a stranger
to his own soul, so that the architecture of his mind falls to
        ruin.

When the voice of her heart rose to heaven pleading re-
        venge for love destroyed, the Lord Olympus
bowed his head; black storms shook water and land upon
        the earth, the skies flung stars out of their courses.

And Theseus, brain deep in midnight, lost forever all that
        he held sacred within his heart. No sign he gave to warn
his father who sleepless with pain (sorrow for his lost son)
        lived for the day
Theseus and his ships sailed into Attic harbours.
Now it is said when Ægeus gave his son to the sea winds, the
        young man no longer resting in the care

of Athena goddess of his city. The king, his arms embracing Theseus said: My son, my son,

you are more precious to me than all the days of my long life
and the few short years that still remain

here for a moment now but gone too soon—all the days and
every hour that you are seaward lost to me I send you
forth against my wisdom,

the future, dark, uncertain. My fate shall be engraved upon
your heart—valorous blood

shall divorce us now, you shall be torn from me yet I shall
hold your image in my eyes

strong as a last gaze westward at the sunset, nor do you leave
me with gladness, I am all sorrow

my white hair is stained with stale earth and dirt; I give you
now a signal for your return.

If you should die then cause this purple scarf and sail to remain at your masthead showing

my grief, but if she, our goddess, who lives in sacred Itonus
defends you

with the same power by which she holds our city, if she (O
fortunate) guides your hand in battle

and the bull's blood flows through your fingers, hold these
things in your mind: let no dreams tarnish them,

these words, bright in your heart, nor time change their
meaning.

108

Soon as your eyes discern our hills, drop then these sails
    dyed with my sorrow,
run a white sheet up your topmast so my joy may discover
    you safe again
and I shall find all happiness I ever knew in that rich glow-
    ing hour that you return.

Theseus had carried these words within his mind as a price-
    less treasure,
but like clouds swept by winds over far mountain tops, they
    vanished;
the father standing alone in a high place, eyes lidless,
    features worn with rivers of tears,
fixed seaward; then came the dark swelling sail that set an
    image of
death in his eyes. He saw fair Theseus dead. He leaped, and
    his frail body mingled with rocks below him.
And Theseus was welcomed by darkened rooms where the
    king's body lay,
Theseus shaken by sorrows deep as the pain he gave to
    Minos's daughter,
daughter of Crete. . . . And she was desolate looking al-
    ways seaward the vision of a vanishing
ship within her heart now and memory of abused love.

And here, set in another corner of the tapestry, rose flower-
    ing Bacchus dancing

and here a company of satyrs, old and young, all with their
  eyes lit, searching the forest
for their Ariadna, fiery with love for her . . .

racing in drunken panic their brains gone mad, lips burst-
  ing with inarticulate cries!
Evoe, Evoe! tossing their shaggy heads. And some threw vine-
  tipped spears and some pitched mangled limbs
of beasts that served as sacrifice to Bacchus, some twined
  snakes round legs, bodies, arms, and some
swung overhead the secret sacred basket filled with the
  mystic tools of ritual
that the curious would give their eyes to see. Some made
  shrill music with the cymbals clanging
and trumpets rang, but the horrible barbarous pipes of
  Bacchus shrieked over all.
These were the characters woven into the spread that covered
  draped seductive loving folds over
this marriage bed.
When the young men of Thessaly had read this legend, eyes
  filled with ancient glory, the gods arrived.
And as the west wind shakes the quiet of waves at dawn and
  morning climbs heavenward toward the sun,
and waves whipped into foam, staccato rhythms, music and
  laughter rising,
and then at last far off on the horizon the light of the sun
  joins the sharp brilliance

of the waves; all's mingled in golden daylight,
so did this company of guests dissolve, leaving halls and the
    estate of this royal palace,
each gone his separate way now all at one with the broad
    countryside.

First came great Chiron from the Pelion hills carrying green
    gifts, flowers from leveled valleys,
and all beautiful things that grow out of the Thessalian hills,
    greenery blossoming
near rivers, these flowers discovered by warm winds that
    drift overland from the fair harbour of Favoni;
and wreaths were there, bright colours and quick fragrance
to fill the palace with sunshine from the hills.

Then there came Peneus from Tempe's valleys, surrounded
    by sweet ferns and lovely nymphs
who move in measures of the Doric dance, nor did he come
    with empty hands; blooming bay trees came with him
roots, branches, trunk, the plane tree and poplar (swaying,
    silver sister of famous Phæthon)
and the tall cypress whose branches pierce the clouds. And
    these he thrust in earth surrounding the palace door-
    way
so that the bride and bridegroom found a home made rich
    with greenery.

Then came Prometheus the prophet with his fading scars
     (flesh torn by rock-chained torture in mid-air).
Then came the father, king of gods with Juno, his wife and
     your sister from the mountain towers of Idrias,
a sister who would not look upon Thetis, nor did she plan to
     celebrate this wedding
only his son, Apollo, left behind.

Now when the gods, relaxed, took ease upon the ivory-footed
     couches and ate a feast from banquet tables,
then came the Fates uttering prophecies, bodies shaken with
     age yet swung in perfect rhythm
of what they sang. All, all in white but for a scarlet hem
     that flowed round thin and yellow with age ankles,
all with red bands (blood against snow) bound round the
     hair.
Never at rest the distaff, gathering wool spins in the left
     hand, the right selecting
strands on five raised fingers, thumb plunging downward, in
     measure to the speed
threads cut by quick teeth and ends of thread and lint dry
     on the lips.
Each syllable rising like a trumpet the Fates sang in one
     voice; and the future,
clear, incontroversial truth rang through the halls:

Master whose government shall rule, bright with immortal
    fame
over Macedonia, a wall of strength—O you shall breed
a son whose name will sound, echoing through time;
this song is truth itself woven by us (the sisters,)
our gift to you this holiday.
Weave, weave and let the spindles run.

O diamond-bright Hesperus arise, pour down your blessings,
under this rain of light the bride comes willingly;
love from her heart in warm blood flowing (her arms
encircling powerful shoulders of you her husband)
floating through the long wedding night.
Weave time, O spindles weave.

There was never a house sheltering love like this love;
never a marriage making two lovers one
as this festival for Peleus and Thetis:
Weave, weave and let the spindles run.

And you shall have a son who knows nor deeds nor words
that make men fall in terror; his enemies
shall never see him turn, they shall see only
his face and breast plunged toward them, feet quick as fire
sped by the wind, fleet as the deer in a broad forest.
Weave time, O spindles weave.

No hero, god or man his equal, even
though Phrygian rivers shall swell with blood
and Pelops (third son of his house) shatter
the walls of Troy in a long wavering war.
Weave, weave and let the spindles run.

This hero's deeds will be a tale recited
by grieving mothers over the bodies of their sons,
white hair undone and frail hands mutilating
their empty breasts:
Weave time, O spindles weave.

Now as the farmer in heat of Summer noon
strikes down before him miles of heavy grain,
his scythe victorious in a golden meadow,
so shall Achilles strike down sons of Troy
in steel-edged battle.
Weave, weave and let the spindles run.

O see him rise, Scamander's wave that conquers
the buried tides; his deeds a monument of dead,
their bodies dam the narrows of Hellespont
whose undercurrents rise warm with the blood
that issues from their wounds
Weave time, O spindles weave.

And even in death on his own funeral pyre
Troy shall be made his victim, his towering

ashes crowned with the white body perishing
the daughter of Troy's king.
Weave, weave and let the spindles run.

And as the Greeks enter the walls of Neptune's city,
then shall Achilles's pyre grow wet with blood
(the kneeling body of Polyxenia
a headless fountain)
Weave time, O spindles weave.

O join your bodies and mingle souls
husband and goddess in deep union love,
this moment is for man and bride.
Weave, weave and let the spindles run.

And when the light of morning pierces night,
the nurse who tends the bride will find that now
the virgin's necklace is no longer worn
by the young matron, nor shall the mother
of the once unmarriagable daughter weep
for lack of grandchildren.
Weave time, O spindles weave.

So sang the sisters of good fortune to Peleus disclosing in
        this fashion what the secret heart
of years held; such was the custom at a hero's wedding be-
        fore religion fell into decay.
In ancient times, resembling human forms, walking as men
        the gods rejoiced in festival on earth

115

Jupiter himself, all radiant, stepped from his shining temple
    and saw on holidays a hundred bulls
struck down to make a feast, a sacrifice of flesh to honour
    him; and Bacchus
strolling down Parnassus saw his worshippers run mad with
    wine and dancing,
capture Delphi, and his sacred altars wreathed in smoke and
    fire.
and there were times when Mars, Athena, and the virgin
    Nemesis came down, directing miles of armed men,
giving them council on the battlefields.

But then followed long years when earth was stained with
    blood and men released their souls to hell, justice
a word forgotten; brothers dipped their fingers into brother's
    blood and sons
no longer wept over a father's body and fathers ripe with
    lust would plan the death
of sons at wedding feasts, their eyes fixed on the bride.
And mothers slept with sons all ignorant, but for a passion
    rising from incestuous crime.
Thus right and wrong became confused; mankind in dark-
    ness, bewildered now ignored the gods.
Never again do gods return to earth or walk with men in the
    bright sun of noon.

WORN with continual grief, Hortalus, grief that divorces me
    from poetry,
I cannot make a festival of words, all flowers and sweet
    voices,
telling how the Muses were conceived, for I am broken in
    a mad sea storm,
I have seen the slowly winding waves of Lethe rise with the
    tide,
have seen them cover his death-silver feet, my brother:
    perishing
underground (O heavy earth of Troy), over him the trem-
    bling shores of
Rhoeteum, eyes cannot penetrate this darkness where he lies.

Never shall I hear the story of your life, speak to you again,
nor see you; more than my soul I loved you, brother, now
my sorrow sings a threnody like the pitiful song flowing
weeping for Itylus out of the dark-shadowed branches of a
    midnight tree.

Out of this sadness Hortalus, I send you these translations of
    the poet Callimachus,
you will know that I have held you in my mind nor shall
    your words
drift to the winds, forgotten,

forgotten as an apple that a girl received in secret from her
   lover,
hid the gift between her breasts, then rose to meet her mother,
(poor girl! for she'd forgotten it)
and the apple fell, see it rolling, freed from her girdle,
while the child stands helpless, glowing red with innocent
   shame.

THIS great astronomer who stares upon the luminous vaults
  of heaven
knew in his heart the time that stars moved in their orbits,
  rising and falling,
light and darkness shifting in broad skies; and when the
  flaming rapid sun vanished
in clear heavens, and at what seasons stars grew small; he
  knew
how the soft voice of love called Trivia out of her chariot of
  heavenly ether
to meet Endymion within the caves of Latmus—
so it was he, great Conon who discovered me a slender thread
  of light, a lock of hair
clipped from the head of Berenice, now gleaming in the
  firmament, a gift sworn
to the goddesses by my mistress who in prayer, hands, white
  arms raised to heaven
pledged me when her royal bridegroom (Egypt's king)
  marched to Assyrian wars.
This was the time when the Egyptian armies conquered the
  Assyrian border lands
and virgins were delivered naked, bleeding, to the Egyptian
  hosts.
Do brides despise her, holy Venus, making a parody of
  parents' tears,

weeping a fountain over the wedding-bed? Yet this is what
    my mistress said when her quick sobs

followed her husband as he marched to war. But these tears
    fell (not alone

for empty bridal bed but for the sad death of a brother).

grief ate at your heart. All the five senses torn from your fair
    body and brain.

Yet you were brave. I have known you as a girl defying
    your mother, and choosing Ptolemy

your lover as a husband, a magnificent show of strength for
    a young virgin.

Yet you were all grief then, a river of tears not to be hidden
    but swept aside

tears coursing through your fingers. O Jupiter! What god had
    worked this change in her?

Then it is true that lovers part in agony. And then, O my
    sweet mistress, then you swore

a sacrifice (me!) to a company of gods if they would promise
    a husband's safe homecoming.

(It was not long before he captured Asia as a province to his
    kingdom)

and now I am fixed in heaven's diadem, your reward to
    heaven for answering your prayers.

I left you most unhappily, clipped from your head my
    queen, and by that head I swear

(by which if anyone swears an empty oath, deserves empty
   rewards)
but who can stand against the strength of steel?
Even the great mountain under the swift course of the sun
was severed by steel and the Medes made a channel to an
   unknown sea
and the young men of Persia sailed their fleet through the
   canal of Athos by strength of steel.
What is a mere strand of hair against this power? O Jupiter
   send a curse down upon Chalybes
who first dug for iron underground and may his children die.
Those who have converted ore to iron bars should perish
   utterly.
All my sisters weep for me. They who saw a brother of
   Memnon float through air to capture me, now mourn
   my loss.
For this bird, servant of the Greek Venus was sent to deliver
   me to her breast.
Then she the goddess decided (me the prize of Berenice's
   sun-bright head) since I,
like Ariadna's crown, was wet with tears, should shine a new-
   born constellation
in the bright firmament; so I was placed with fiery Venus at
   one side and Callisto (the Bear) upon the other;
I guided tardy Bootes in his late course into his midnight
   Ocean.

Even though I move in company with gods by night and then
    at dawn mingle with nymphs in the sea wave,
(O Nemesis though stars destroy me with angry speech, I do
    not fear to tell what's in my heart)
I have no joy in my good fortune. I long for my dear mis-
    tress and the home where thousands of times
I drank perfume (O divine ambrosia) that watered me.
O virgins when the marriage torch throws its golden light
    upon you
and with naked breasts erect you meet your husbands, re-
    member me and let me share the ointment
that is spread over your chaste bodies. (But those who stain
    their beds with adultery let all
the dainties of their toilet flow into a thirsty sewer
merely a drink for dust in gutters.) I tell you O my virgin
    brides to live in holy chastity.
And you my mistress when you gaze starward at midnight,
    send your prayers to Venus with an offering
of perfume to your slave, for I am held here by the stars
    and lonely
I long for my sweet Berenice, my Queen. Let Orion and
    Aquaris
flaming guard the heavens, let me return to her I love.

HERE'S my greeting, door, Jove bless you! once the friendly
　　servant of a becoming husband and his aged father,
they say that you were an honest friend to the old man,
　　Balbus,
but now he's dead and underground—and you a malicious
　　slave to his young son,
guard his marriage bed indifferently. And some say you no
　　longer serve your master
with admirable courtesy, your faithfulness (once perfect)
　　now infirm.

But it's no fault of mine (my duty's now to praise a strange
　　young man Caecilius) no one can say
that I've done wrong, yet everyone is shouting: look at that
　　door, count all his crimes; if there is evil,
blame him.

What you say here proves nothing—give me the facts so I
　　can see them or feel them move my blood.

What shall I say and who shall question me?

I do. And if you have a story, I am here.

If you have heard my mistress was a virgin in her husband's
　　arms, it is a lie. Here's the first fact, the poor young fool

had a poor foolish member of no use to a wife, for it would
   never
raise his tunic. But the young man's father took the girl to
   bed,
a pervert in his own home, breeding incest,
some say his mad old brains were hot with love and some
   say
that the fluid of life in him was always sterile, paralysing his
   own son, her husband,
and yet his nerves were fed by lust and he was fit to teach
   the girl how not to be a virgin.

Here was a pious father! Look at him, making his own son a
   cuckold. Noble old man!

And this is not all the story, for down at Brixia, behind the
   hills of China where the sweet golden melo flows
(Brixia beloved mother of Verona) they tell how this young
   bride has often slept adulterously
with Postumius and lay languishing within the arms of young
   Cornelius.

Some one will raise this question: How is it that a door shall
   hear this gossip,
since a door fixed to his master's threshold, cannot hear

all that is said, you merely open and guard the way into
    your master's house.

My answer's this: I heard my mistress whispering to her
    maids, these stories of her incest—
she had no mind for me, a helpless door (she thought) has
    neither ears
nor tongue—and further: there is someone I will not name
    because
his anger would flame from a terrible forehead, he
is tall (this gentleman of hers) and once, O long ago,
a court of law brought a false charge against him, named
    him the father
of a bastard child.

HERE is your letter, stained with tears; I see how time and
    an embittered fortune

had thrown their weight upon you and how a storm destroyed
    your hopes and left you shipwrecked

calling me to save you from disaster, a man now in the
    shadow of death's door,

sleepless in a widower's bed, while sacred Venus

tortures your limbs; unseeing, you gaze at the words written
    by ancient poets,

then your mind, wandering, encircles grief again; awake,
    you stare at poetry and beauty fades.

Now by this letter you have made my friendship humble
    with gratitude,

for you have called me friend in this dark hour, longed for
    my poetry, fruit of my genius and love.

Rather than have you think me careless of duties fallen to
    friendship, know that I'm in misery

struck by the same sea storm that overwhelmed you and my
    poetry fails;

nor shall you find happiness in what I say. O Manlius,

when I was young, a spring tree flowering, all dressed in
    white,

my poetry held laughter and love embraced and I was not
    unknown

to the bright goddess and muse who mingles bitterness with
sweet melodies.

All this, once mine, lies in the sepulture that holds my
brother's body, O my brother,

you have darkened my mind; the house, the family that
bears my name destroyed, its ruins fallen

within your grave.

When you were living my joy in life delighted you, but now
there is no passion

within the blood that feeds my brain; love and the songs of
love are silent, O my brother.

Now Manlius, when you write that I am sleeping here in
Verona,

and that young men in Rome warm frozen members between
my sheets and she is faithless to me—

I say here's no dishonour, Manlius—I am not weak, but
sorrow

conquers me and all that I may give you (friendship, love)
devoured by grief. I cannot send you

new poetry or old. My manuscript's in Rome, where I have
lived and shall return.

I've nothing with me here, except a few short poems but none
of these would please you;

nor has my mind grown small, nor my affections narrow.
You would be welcome to

the best, all that I have to offer.

O GODDESSES of poetry, hear me now, nothing can check
   my flow of words to tell you how

Allius served me. By these lines I shall preserve his name,
   defying the swift course of time against the darkest

night where the years fall forgotten. Here is the story of his
   kindness, hardihood,

that you must tell again, recite his deeds to thousands, and
   make these words live, written

for posterity, and stand indelible upon an ancient scroll.

*   *   *   *   *   *   *   *

And may his fame grow large and larger, magnified by
   death, nor shall time, the spider, weave

a slow veil over the forgotten name of Allius, a signature in
   bronze.

You already know how Venus, goddess hermaphrodite, with
   double trickery and by what means had ruined me,

until my eyes a river ran storming down my features, all of
   me on fire like the flames of Etna burning

or like smoking waters that boil and steam hard by Ther-
   mopylæ.

Allius was welcome to me as the brilliant stream that flows
   from mountain tops over green rocks falling,

a silver thread through deep rich valleys following a course
   through peopled villages and towns

and winding into earth, split by the heat of sun where trav-
ellers, weary, stoop to drink; you are my saviour,

Allius, like the relief after a black storm that comes to salt
wave baffled sailors in a gentle wind risen out of their
prayers to Castor Pollux.

All this to me are you, my Allius,

who gave me entrance to a field where nothing grew but walls
built high against me, then you lead the way

into a house and to its mistress where all could follow the
demands of love! there where I found my lady,

white, shining goddess! and I heard her foot (slender and
luminous) fall on the threshold.

She was Laodamia, come to life again, still burning with immortal love to meet Protesilaus in a house already
doomed,

(for his blood the blood of martyrdom, the lords of heaven
have not made holy, even to this day)

Lady of Rhamnusia, templed Nemesis, O may I never do
anything that stands against the laws

of heaven. See how the altar drinks the blood of martyrs, its
deep thirst known by Laodamia

who saw her husband sacrificed. Her arms were torn from
him before she learned how to endure a life of lone-
liness;

no winter nights were hers to satisfy the passion of love
　　　within her veins, for he was taken
a warrior (not as the fates had promised) to fall before the
　　　walls of Ilium—
and this because Troy brought upon herself the wrath of
　　　Greece and fiery warriors
marching down for the recapture of Helen raped. O mur-
　　　derous Troy! the sepulture
of Europe, Asia, the open grave of heroes who had died too
　　　soon. Troy's earth devoured,
(O miserable death) my brother, O my brother, my light,
　　　the shining name, the house that gave us birth, de-
　　　stroyed,
all perishing, (everything that bloomed when you walked
　　　forth upon the earth) now sunken
underground, mould in a grave. And you are many miles
　　　from home, your ashes mingling
with foreign dust, far, far from the remains of those who
　　　gave you birth; thrust underground
remote alone, dishonoured by the soil of adulterous Troy!
And then, joined by a common cause, the youth of Greece
　　　left homes and firesides,
left all they loved behind them, the marching feet of war
　　　sounding within
the quiet room where Paris slept with Helen.

By this mad turn of fortune, O Laodamia, beautiful bride,
   you gave your husband (sweeter than life and soul)
to darkness. Yet your love ran deeper, a strong current winding, following a course
deeper than the gulf (so have Greek poets sung) that Hercules, Amphitryon's son (fathered perhaps,
by Jove himself) made, excavating mountain-sides, to carve
   a bottomless subterranean channel
draining the marshes near Cyllenian Pheneus.
And striking deep within the hollowed hills, he conquered
   monstrous winged beasts, made them the means by
   which
Hebe was freed from maidenhood and a new demi-god entered the gates of heaven.
But deeper than these subterranean caves, O Laodamia, was
   your deep love that gave you strength to bear
unbroken the yoke of widowed tragedy.
Yet from this marriage (all too brief) a child, nursed by the
   only daughter
of a father struck helpless by old age; but by this late-born
   child
freed from the rapacious hands of heirs desiring his death.
   These vultures turned aside from his
poor body, and the child received his blessing.

Never did a dove find pleasure in her snow-white lover (even
though the dove moves with fierce abandon

into embraces more passionate than any woman born, beyond
the pain of kisses that draw blood)

than you discovered in your golden husband.

As glorious a love as yours (or very nearly so) was that
brought to me by my light, my love, who came into my
arms

like you, bright lady of an ancient fable.

She came with Cupid dancing, his golden scarves circling
behind her.

And though Catullus cannot be her only lover, nor can he
satisfy the wealth of her desires,

forgive her these few brief kisses set upon the lips of other
men, our love shall not go staring blind

with idiot jealousy. Juno herself forgave all-passionate Jove
curbing her anger against his faithlessness,

but since men cannot be compared with gods . . .

* * * * * * * *

and we shall thrust aside the intolerant rage of a trembling
old man, the father,

for this lady came not from her father's hands into these
rooms sweet with Assyrian odours

but in soft midnight, giving me her miracles of love, a gift
now stolen from her husband's heart.

This is my pleasure (enough for one glorious day) and she
     will engrave its history
in the calendar of our love with a white stone.

So let these verses be my gift to you, Allius, and time shall
     never
cover your name with rust; may the gods give you justice and
     all good things in life and come like ancient Themis to
     your side
(as in the days long gone, he once delivered rewards to
     men who lived in honest piety).
May you be happy with that (O luminous) girl: in this house
     where we found voiceless, inexplicable joy. May good
     fortune fall upon the mistress
of this place and he who laid the stones for us to walk upon,
and above all I praise this lady, this girl, my love, this light
     that changes midnight into day
and in whose life I live.

6 9

HERE'S no mystery, friend Rufus. You say that girls will
  never
leap between your thighs, your arms, delightfully, not even
if you try to make them perverts with fine clothes and a
  gift of
rare and dainty jewelry.

All your charms, my Rufus, are killed by this mad rumour:
there's something of a goat about your person (so they
  whisper)
perhaps a fearful odour that's wild and strong, a warning
that would terrify
anyone. You are a goat. No wonder
girls will run away when they think of sleeping
with a filthy animal. Take my advice, friend Rufus,
destroy the beast. He does you harm and girls will not embrace him
as a sweet bedfellow.

MY woman says that she would rather wear the wedding-veil
    for me
than anyone: even if Jupiter himself came storming after
    her;
that's what she says, but when a woman talks to a hungry,
ravenous lover, her words should be written upon the wind
and engraved in rapid waters.

MY friend, your rival (if anyone) deserves the curses that
    have fallen upon him,

for the smell of a goat leaps from his armpits and he is woe-
    fully lamed by fiery sciatica.

But here's a double miracle: since he has inherited your dis-
    eases

when he sleeps with your lady she faints away (killed maybe)
    by the vicious

goat hidden in his arms, while he, poor bastard, lies im-
    potent, weak with the frantic pain

rising from his sciatica.

72

THERE was a time, O Lesbia, when you said Catullus was
    the only man on earth who could understand you,
who could twine his arms round you, even Jove himself less
    welcome.
And when I thought of you, my dear, you were not the mere
    flesh and
the means by which a lover finds momentary rapture.
My love was half paternal, as a father greets his son or
smiles at his daughter's husband.

Although I know you well (too well), my love now turns
    to fire
and you are small and shallow.
Is this a miracle? Your wounds in love's own battle
have made me your companion, perhaps, a greater lover,
but O, my dear, I'll never be
the modest boy who saw you as a lady, delicate and sweet,
a paragon of virtue.

LOOK for no gratitude, tolerance, or respect anywhere on
    earth
nor place your hopes in man, for everything is lost:
If you are generous, expect no answer and no return for
    generosity.
All goodness fails.

Look at me now, sunken with a great sorrow in my soul,
but there is nothing in life so bitter
as the betrayal of friendship by someone who yesterday
was my one and only friend.

THERE came a time when Gellius heard that his uncle, stern,
  pious, censorious,

issued an order: there was to be no talk of lechery in his
  house,

no fornication within its walls. So Gellius set to work,

slept with his uncle's wife and the doomed man could say
  nothing;

Gellius had changed him into an Egyptian god, carved out of
  stone and noted for his silence.

And now if Gellius were to practise nimble tricks of pederasty upon him,

the poor devil would not dare to say a word,

not even a whisper.

7 5

YOU are the cause of this destruction, Lesbia,
that has fallen upon my mind;
this mind that has ruined itself
by fatal constancy.
And now it cannot rise from its own misery
to wish that you become
best of women, nor can it fail
to love you even though all is lost and you destroy
all hope.

IF man can find rich consolation, remembering his good deeds
    and all he has done,

if he remembers his loyalty to others, nor abuses his religion
    by heartless betrayal

of friends to the anger of powerful gods,

then, my Catullus, the long years before you shall not sink
    in darkness with all hope gone,

wandering, dismayed, through the ruins of love.

All the devotion that man gives to man, you have given,
    Catullus,

your heart and your brain flowed into a love that was deso-
    late, wasted, nor can it return.

But why, why do you crucify love and yourself through the
    years?

Take what the gods have to offer and standing serene, rise
    forth as a rock against darkening skies;

and yet you do nothing but grieve, sunken deep in your
    sorrow, Catullus,

for it is hard, hard to throw aside years lived in poisonous
    love that has tainted your brain

and must end.

If this seems impossible now, you must rise

to salvation. O gods of pity and mercy, descend and witness
    my sorrow, if ever

you have looked upon man in his hour of death, see me now
    in despair.

Tear this loathsome disease from my brain. Look, a subtle
    corruption has entered my bones,

no longer shall happiness flow through my veins like a river.
    No longer I pray

that she love me again, that her body be chaste, mine forever.

Cleanse my soul of this sickness of love, give me power to
    rise, resurrected, to thrust love aside,

I have given my heart to the gods, O hear me, omnipotent
    heaven,

and ease me of love and its pain.

RUFUS, I have given the best of all I am to you, thrown
    it away, for it has fallen through your fingers,
(all wasted? No, something, perhaps, for you. I paid a
    ruinous price for your dead friendship;
you had broken your way into my very soul, tearing at my
    entrails, your hands upon my soul itself).
Look, my life has been left empty and good fortune vanishes
    with you.
You are the curse that falls upon the grave of all I love and
    all that's dear to me.

             * * * * * * * *
             * * * * * * * *

Eh, what grieves me now is the thought of your saliva,
diseased, and poisoning the lips of a young virgin.
Yet this is certain, you
shall not escape disaster—
men will recite your name, your crimes shall be a legend
to countless generations.

GALLUS has brothers (so I've heard,) one owns a lovely
    wife and the
other, what a lovely son he has to offer.

Gallus, the fine fellow, with an eye for beauty
knows how to put a lovely boy to bed with (O how clever!)
a passionate, lovely woman.

But this Gallus is a fool, see him as he teaches
the boy that incest is delight, recreation for gay
young men.

Gallus is blind, forgetting that his wife's a comely woman.

LESBIUS is beautiful. And why? Lesbia loves him.
Loves him more than you and your family, Catullus,
for he is the flower of an ancient lineage.

Since he is delicate, refined, he'd sell your relatives
and you, my dear Catullus,
as slaves to buy the kisses of three boys if they've the courage
to taste his vile saliva.

O GELLIUS why are your red lips like snow
when you arise from sleep either in morning sunlight,
or when you wake after a long nap at noon.

Then all these stories that they tell of your perversions
are truth itself;
look at his buttocks, see how they've been abused;
witness his lips, they are still moist with evidence of
worse crimes.

IN all this city Juventius is there no one
who'd make a lover for you—no man other than this sweet
    boy,
this creature from the plague-struck streets of Pesaro
this thing of stone, merely a statue paler
than gold? He's in your heart; look he is more to you
than I am.
You have no knowledge of what you do or what your actions
    mean, O Juventius!

QUINTIUS do you want Catullus to be in debt to you
for the use of his two eyes? or something that means more
    to him
than these two eyes could ever look upon?
Then, do not dare walk off with this that's more
than his eyes are to him, nor take away
anything, everything
more valuable than sight to any man.

LESBIA speaks evil of me with her husband near and he
(damned idiot) loves to hear her.

Chuckling, the fool is happy, seeing nothing, understanding
nothing.

If she forgetting me fell silent, her heart would be his alone,
content and peaceful;

but she raves, spitting hatred upon me, all of which carries
this meaning:

I am never out of her mind, and what is more, she rises in
fury against me

with words that make her burn, her blood passionate for me.

ARRIUS, when he tries to speak of Justice, says the word

with so much stress on the first letter that the syllables are
      murdered, no justice from his lips:

and "Treachery" is Treachery indeed when he pronounces it.

Most likely his mother taught him, uncle, grandfather, grand-
      mother all recited these words as he does now,

each sure to teach him how to speak a language above his
      station.

O what refinement! When he was sent to Syria, our ears were
      free of him, and we were glad

to hear again our own sweet, flowing syllables—

but here's bad news, the creature is returning

by way of the Ionian sea and now the waves, even these inno-
      cent waves will be

Hionian forever.

85

I HATE and love.

    And if you ask me why,
I have no answer, but I discern,
can feel, my senses rooted in eternal torture.

86

THERE are many who think of Quintia in terms of beauty,
but to me she is merely tall and golden white, erect,
and I admit each of these separate distinctions in her favour,
yet I object, deny,
that the word "beauty" describes her person;
for she has no charm, not even a grain of salt in her whole
    body
to give you appetite—
now Lesbia has beauty, she is everything
that's handsome, glorious,
and she has captured all that Venus has to offer
in ways of love.

NO woman, if she is honest, can say that she's
been blessed with greater love, my Lesbia,
than I have given you;
nor has any man held to a contract made
with more fidelity
than I have shown, my dear,
in loving you.

88

EH, what is Gellius up to now, awake all night long, his
   tunic open
for the delight of his mother and sister?
And what is the fantastic meaning
behind cuckolding his uncle, not allowing the man to be a
   proper husband?
Doesn't this fellow Gellius know that he has covered his
   person
with the filth of countless crimes, that he's
scrofulous with indelible lecheries?
(All the rivers, lakes and oceans of the world, even
Oceanus and his wife could never wash you clean, O
   Gellius!)
And if Gellius (head lowered) practised gymnastic fornication
upon himself—why here's another pastime. There is no
   crime
too great for him.

89

GELLIUS looks a bit worn. And why not? He has a ripe,
    lusty mother to play with
and a lively young sister, to say nothing of a generous uncle
    and any
number of sweet little girls always ready for him at all hours.
And why shouldn't he be slender and languid forever? O
    even if he
did nothing but finger his——(though no man touches his
    own) you will find
this is merely one reason (no doubt there are many) why
Gellius is lean.

LET them conceive a child, these two, Gellius and his mother,

from their dark sighs and kisses let them make a priest

out of their devilish love-making at all hours.

And if the legends about the Persians are true,

then let the child be born a Persian priest glib with holy
soothsaying,

son of mother and son, torn from the womb, worshipping the
gods,

melting the veil from his eyes and the spew of after-birth

in the flames of the altar.

91

O GELLIUS I once had hopes that you would not betray me,
  me surrounded by this evil, disastrous love
that conquered me. I did not know you well, I thought (this
  was a dream) that you could somehow
force your mind to check your crimes. But then I saw that
  she whose love was fire to my blood
had welcomed you and she was not your mother or your
  sister,
and I was joined to you unwillingly in intimate relationship.
This gave you evil satisfaction and you enjoy, better than all
  things on earth,
love that is stripped of love and is merely crime.

92

LESBIA, forever spitting fire at me, is never silent. And now
if Lesbia fails to love me, I shall die. Why
do I know in truth her passion burns for me? Because I am
    like her,
because I curse her endlessly. And still, O hear me gods,
I love her.

93

I SHALL not raise my hand to please you, Caesar,
nor do I care if you are white or black.

HIS very name suggests adultery, most certainly
it is Mentula.
And it is often said soup-greens are grown
to fill the pot.

CINNA, my friend, after nine years of harvest and long
    winter
has given us his poem while Hortensius has written
(at least) five hundred thousand poems in one. . . .

Smyrna, the work of Cinna will find its way beyond the rivers
    of Crete where it was born.
But this, the Annals of Volusius will die here on the river
    Padua,
and the paper on which they're written serve as covering
    carelessly enough for fish
that's sold in city streets. I praise these lines now published
    by my friend,
they shall ring immortal music in my blood,
the mob may follow where they will
and glory in their favorite poet, Antimachus.

9 6

IF anything can pierce impenetrable earth and echo in the
    silence
of the grave, my Calvus, it is our sad memory
of those we love. (Our longing for them makes them bloom
    again,
quickened with love and friendship,
even though they left us long ago, heavy with tears).
Surely, your Quintilia now no longer cries against powerful
    death
(who had taken her away from you too soon and she was
    gone).
Look she is radiant, fixed in your mind, happy forever.

COME, does it matter if I greet his buttocks or his head,
this creature Æmilius. Perhaps his buttocks are more
   friendly, they conceal no teeth.
Look at his mouth, foul with disease, teeth broken as the
   broken wheel of an old wagon
patched by a mule's hide. Yet he is active in the game of
   love, let him return
to slavery. A woman who would sleep with him would sleep
   with any
rancid slave who'd give her body satisfaction.

98

O VICTIUS you stink.

You if any man has earned what may be said

against fools and bloated windbags, Victius.

Go, use your tongue to some good purpose, clean the back-
sides

and the boots of slaves who stand in gutters

with this tongue of yours. You'd kill us all, your enemies—

but not a word, open your mouth (O what an odour, Victius!)

and we'll fall dead.

99

WHILE you were at the games, intent upon
playing your part, O lovely Juventius,
I stole a kiss from you, a kiss far sweeter
than that sweet wine that the immortals drink,
feasting forever.
But I was caught, discovered,
and for an eternal hour my soul and body pierced,
crucified, and all my tears were useless.
For you were angry and in your fashion,
utterably cruel. You washed your hands
and lips at once, the symbol of our marriage
washed away as though your lips were stained by some
     disease
caught from a bitch. And what is more
your quick magnificent rage has made me prisoner
of love for you and this immortal kiss
both sweet and rancid, bitter as hellebore.
Since this is what you've given me
in return for love (a miserable love) no more shall I
(even in play) torture my soul
with stolen kisses.

100

CÆLIUS is desperately in love with Aufilenius,
Quintius would surrender his life to Aufilena
(these two men the flower of their families in Verona)
Here's the golden age of brotherhood, now risen again and
     blooming—
one or the other claims my favour.

Then, you, my Cælius,
take all I have; you've shown me that your friendship
served mine. And at a time when Love, fire in my blood, con-
     sumed me.
Here's good fortune, Cælius! May your true love prosper.

DEAR brother, I have come these many miles, through strange lands to this Eastern Continent

to see your grave, a poor sad monument of what you were, O brother.

And I have come too late; you cannot hear me; alone now I must speak

to these few ashes that were once your body and expect no answer.

I shall perform an ancient ritual over your remains, weeping,

(this plate of lentils for dead men to feast upon, wet with my tears)

O brother, here's my greeting: here's my hand forever welcoming you

and I forever saying: good-bye, good-bye.

102

WHATEVER is told to me, Cornelius, as the deep confidence
of a faithful friend, you will soon discover
that I deposit his words in sepultures within my mind
and I am silence itself
inspiring awe like that stone god, Harpocrates,
the Egyptian.

1 0 3

WHAT arrogance Silo, and what dignity!
Come, give me back my ten pieces of gold,
(the girl was neat; I paid you for her)
or would you rather keep the money? But leave me now,
no more of your big words; take all your arrogance,
threats and thunder outside—and
close the door.

COME, do you think that I'd be making an evil story
out of my very life, speaking ill of her
who's more to me than my two eyes; I could not,
even if I did not love her desperately; but you—
drinking and talking to that poor fool Tappo,
could build somehow (and out of wind and rain)
a world of monsters.

MENTULA, poet now! half kills himself climbing the hills of Pipla where the muses stride; and seeing him, seize their pitchforks, toss him to earth again.

106

YOU see a pretty boy out walking with an auctioneer,
both arm in arm,
and you suspect that this young man has a quick eye for trade
and sells himself.

WHEN at last after long despair, our hopes ring true again
and long-starved desire eats, O then the mind leaps in the
    sunlight—Lesbia
so it was with me when you returned. Here was a treasure
more valuable than gold; you, whom I love beyond hope,
    giving yourself
to me again. That hour, a year of holidays, radiant,
where is the man more fortunate than I,
where can he find anything in life more glorious
than the sight of all his wealth restored?

108

IF, O Cominius, your grey hair is stained with the dark
     colours of an evil life,
and you are put to death, the people rising against you,
no doubt your tongue, offensive to all good
men, shall be extracted, cut up and fed to vultures,
then your eyes shall be dug forth and served as food to ease
     a raven's throat
and dogs will eat your entrails,
the rest of you, scattered limbs and odd detail,
will make a dinner for stray wolves.

109

MY life, my love, you say our love will last forever;
O gods remember
her pledge, convert the words of her avowal into a prophecy.
Now let her blood speak, let sincerity govern each syllable
    fallen
from her lips, so that the long years of our lives shall be
a contract of true love inviolate
against time itself, a symbol of eternity.

110

AN honest girl, Aufilena, an artist at her trade of love,
will find her man (pleased by her services) ready
to pay her well, gracing her labours
with praise and no small share of his possessions.

Expecting much from you
lady
(O what promises you made) I paid you gloriously
and now, retiring, you vanish,
transformed, I warn you (once my friend), into my
enemy.
Convert your person into honest gold, or, if you will,
become austere and pure. My Aufilena, but remember
this:
my money's gone; and you in taking it are worse
than the established common breed of whores waiting for
men at night
on dark street corners.

111

THERE is no greater honour, Aufilena, than to be
    known
as a chaste wife,
yet it is better to be called a common whore
than to bear and raise your uncle's children.

112

NASO, you're a man's man, and yet there are not many
men who would care to play at being what you are to many
  men—
to go at full length downward, Naso,
everything to many men, and homosexual.

CINNA, during the early days of the first consulship of
    Pompey,
two women received the duties of a husband from this
    Mæcilla:
again our Pompey's counsel and these women
are still at work, but add three cyphers after the figure 2,
and you will have two thousands.
O adultery! You breed beyond all reason.

COME, there can be no doubt that this Mentula
owns property at Fermo, a magnificent
estate with rare birds, fishes, wide fields of grain
and rich, rolling meadows, merely a wealthy landscape,
so far beyond his income that he's poor,
and he is rich only in minus quantities;
the place is eloquent with mortgages.
If praise consoles a man who needs a house
wherein to sleep, come, let us praise Mentula,
and his thriving acres.

MENTULA has thirty acres of meadow land, swamps,
and forty acres fit for cultivation,
all in one piece.
Crœsus himself might envy him,—look at the wealth here:
soil for raising vegetables, land for grazing cattle,
and the sea itself, extending far beyond our continents,
disappears, far North, a frozen river.
This is a miracle, and he, Mentula
(not human as we are) becomes a giant,
towering over us.

CXVI

SAEPE tibi studioso animo uenante requirens
   carmina uti possem mittere Battiadae,
qui te lenirem nobis, neu conarere
   telis infestum mittere in usque caput,
hunc uideo mihi nunc frustra sumptum esse laborem,
   Gelli, nec nostras hic ualuisse preces.
contra nos tela ista tua euitamus amictei:
   at fixus nostris tu dabi supplicium.

I HAVE searched the corners of my mind, O Gellius,
to find a way to make myself attractive
and to your liking. I sent you poems
written by Callimachus—and still your arrows stormed my
     head, our war continued.
My truce has come to nothing, Gellius.
Now, with my cloak wrapped round my arm in self-defense
I'll give you war again, my arrows piercing
your naked body.

NOTES TO THE TRANSLATIONS

36th Stanza—Here is a deliberate anachronism; but "toilet paper" seems to be an apt definition of *cacata carta*.

37th Stanza—"Roadhouse," even though it has the character of an anachronism, is perhaps the best means by which the connotations of *Salax taberna* may be conveyed to the modern reader.

41st Stanza—In the fourth line, reference is made to the spendthrift of Formiae. Catullus was evidently thinking of Mamurra.

43rd Stanza—As in 41 we have another reference to Mamurra.

51st Stanza—There have been many arguments over the disposition of the fourth stanza. The first three stanzas are part of the famous translation of Sappho. The last stanza is Catullus's own.

68th (a) and 68th (b) Stanza—The first forty-one lines of this poem are in the form of a letter to a friend, Manlius. The rest of the poem is a tribute to Allius—usually regarded as a separate poem.

77th Stanza—The asterisks denote the possibility of these two fragments being part of the same poem.

101st Stanza—"through strange lands to this Eastern Continent" implies that Catullus crossed seas as well as travelled overland.
The ritual referred to in the poem is one in which a plate of eggs, lentils, or salt is given as an offering to the dead. Here, as elsewhere, I have interpolated an explanation of a ritual for the sake of making the image clear to the modern reader.